Ahmad
Ahmad

OUTCOMES

BEGINNER
STUDENT'S BOOK AND WORKBOOK

HUGH DELLAR
ANDREW WALKLEY

SPLIT EDITION A

1 BE

IN THIS UNIT YOU LEARN HOW TO:
- introduce yourself and other people
- understand simple questions with *be*
- answer questions with one or two words
- use numbers to say prices and times
- order in a coffee shop
- say the order is wrong

page 6

2 LIVE, WORK, EAT

- ask and say where you live
- ask about someone's job
- talk about people you know
- understand a menu
- say what you like / don't like
- answer a waiter and order food

page 14

VIDEO 1: People page 22   REVIEW 1: page 23

3 LOVE, WANT, NEED

- ask how things are
- respond to good and bad news
- use adjectives to describe things
- ask and talk about things people have
- ask someone to repeat

page 24

4 WHERE AND WHEN?

- ask about places and say what's there
- understand simple directions
- talk about your week
- ask for help / ask to do things in class

page 32

VIDEO 2: Morning page 40   REVIEW 2: page 41

5 GOING PLACES

- talk about good places to go
- say how to get to places
- talk about journeys
- buy train tickets
- ask about and say your plans
- say where and when to meet

page 42

6 AWAY FROM HOME

- say there's a problem
- say *don't worry* and *that's OK*
- ask how something was
- check in to a hotel
- talk about your stay
- ask what people did

page 50

VIDEO 3: Ancient land page 58   REVIEW 3: page 59

GRAMMAR	VOCABULARY	READING	LISTENING	DEVELOPING CONVERSATIONS
• 'm, 's, 're • Questions with *be* • *his, her, our, their* • *not*	• Numbers 1–12 • People • Numbers 13–22 • Question words • Times and prices • In a coffee shop	• Invitations	• Meeting people and introducing yourself • Ordering in a coffee shop	• Checking names • Ordering and serving drinks
• Present simple • Present simple questions: *do you* • Present simple: *don't (do not)* • Plural / no plural • *like / don't like*	• My home • Jobs • Food and drinks	• The world in one city	• Where do you live? • Ordering in a restaurant	• *And you?* • Ordering food
• Negatives with *be* • Present simple: *doesn't* • Present simple questions: *does* • *a* and *any*	• Adjectives • *go, take, want* • Things	• What do people want?	• Asking how things are	• Responding to news • Asking for help in conversation
• *Is there ...? / There's ...* • Adverbs of frequency • *Can ...?*	• Places • Days and times of day • Classroom verbs	• The end of the working week	• Giving directions	• *called*
• *Are there ...? / There are ...* • Talking about plans: *I'm/We're going* • Asking about plans: *going* and *doing*	• Getting there • Buying tickets	• Why I love train travel	• Talking about good places to go • Talking about plans	• *best* • *Where are you going?* • *I'll meet you*
• Past simple: common irregular verbs • Regular past simple endings • Past simple negatives • Past simple questions	• Problems • Hotels and checking in	• A holiday in Costa Rica	• Meeting a friend at the airport • A conversation in a hostel	• *Don't worry / That's OK*

Grammar reference pages 60–72   **Regular and irregular verbs page 74**   **Vocabulary reference pages 75–79**
Information files pages 80–82   **Audio scripts pages 83–93**

SPLIT EDITION B

IN THIS UNIT YOU LEARN HOW TO:

7 GOING OUT AND STAYING IN

- talk about activities you like
- say what you like doing or prefer
- talk about books, TV and music
- talk about people and things from other countries
- talk about clothes you want to buy
- ask and give opinions

8 HERE AND THERE

- talk about what people are doing
- explain why someone isn't there
- talk about houses and rooms
- ask about things you can't find
- talk about working at home

VIDEO 4: Bike riding in Utah   REVIEW 4

9 HEALTHY AND HAPPY

- talk about health and problems
- ask people if they are better
- talk about what's important in a country or society
- talk about small and large quantities
- talk about how you know people
- ask about places people have been to

10 NEWS

- talk about the weather
- tell people about future plans and predictions
- say what's happening near you
- make plans with other people
- talk about some simple news stories
- ask questions about the news

VIDEO 5: A special skill   REVIEW 5

11 LIFE AND HISTORY

- talk about celebrations and events
- invite people and reply
- talk about dates and when things happen
- talk about your life
- take part in a guided tour
- ask questions about people and places

12 THANK YOU AND GOODBYE

- tell someone a problem
- offer solutions and say thank you
- explain purpose
- talk about gifts
- tell people what to do
- say goodbye

VIDEO 6: Diwali   REVIEW 6

GRAMMAR	VOCABULARY	READING	LISTENING	DEVELOPING CONVERSATIONS
• like + -ing • Present continuous: *I'm* and *are you ... ?* • *this/these, one/ones*	• Words for activities • Country adjectives • Buying clothes	• Are you a big reader?	• Talking about activities you like • Talking about what you are doing • Buying new clothes	• *Me too* and *I prefer* • Opinions
• Present continuous: all forms • Personal pronouns	• Collocations • In the house • Verbs and people	• Homeworkers	• Where are they? • Talking about something you lost	• Sending messages • *maybe*
• Time phrases for the past • Quantity	• Bad health and accidents • Country and society • Meeting and moving	• Iceland: possibly the best country in the world	• Talking about health and problems • Talking about how you know people	• *Are you feeling better?* • *Have you been ...?*
• Future: *am/are/is going* • Past forms review	• Summer and winter • Entertainment • National and international news	• A year of fun in one weekend	• Talking about the weather	• *I think so / I don't think so* • Deciding what to do
• Questions review • Explaining when: time phrases • Explaining why: *because* and *so*	• Months • Life events • History	• A changed life: John Bird • A very short history of Suwon Hwaseong	• Talking about future events and inviting people • Asking a tour guide questions	• Invitations
• *I'll* • Explaining purpose: *for* or *to* • Telling people to do things: imperatives	• Offering solutions • Leaving and saying goodbye	• How to give better gifts	• Offering solutions	• Checking and thanking

IN THIS UNIT YOU LEARN HOW TO:
- introduce yourself and other people
- understand simple questions with *be*
- answer questions with one or two words
- use numbers to say prices and times
- order in a coffee shop
- say the order is wrong

1 ▶1 Listen to the numbers.

1	one	5	five	9	nine
2	two	6	six	10	ten
3	three	7	seven	11	eleven
4	four	8	eight	12	twelve

2 ▶1 Listen again. Repeat the numbers.

WORDS FOR UNIT 1

3 Look at the words and photos.

1	**hus**band and **wife**	7	that's **right**
2	**what**?	8	fresh **o**range **juice**
3	**So**rry!	9	have **lunch**
4	a **ba**by **boy**	10	I don't **know**!
5	**tea** with **milk**	11	the **num**ber 19 **bus**
6	**food** and **drink**	12	a big **flat**

4 ▶2 Listen and repeat the words.

5 Work in pairs. Don't look at the words.

Student A: say the number.

Student B: say the word(s).

Unit 1 Be 7

NICE TO MEET YOU

LISTENING

1 ▶ 3 Listen to the conversation.

Teacher: What's your name?
Student: Lara.
Teacher: Hi. I'm Greg.
Student: Nice to meet you.
Teacher: Yes. You too.

2 ▶ 4 Listen and repeat.
　1 **What's** your **name**?
　2 **Nice** to **meet** you.

3 Practise the conversation from Exercise 1 with other students. Say your names.

4 ▶ 5 Listen to Khalid introduce Lara and Dom.

Khalid: Lara, this is my friend Dom.
Lara: Hi. Nice to meet you.
Dom: Yes. You too.

5 Work in groups. Introduce other students.

DEVELOPING CONVERSATIONS

Checking names
A: *Who's she?*
B: *Aretha Franklin.*

A: *Who **are they**?*
B: ***I don't know.***

A: *Who**'s he**?*
B: *I don't know.*

6 Look at the people in File 1 on page 80. Check the names.

7 Work in pairs. Say all the names in the class.
　A: *Lara, Khalid, ... Who's she?*
　B: *I don't know. He's Joan. Who's he?*

8

VOCABULARY People

8 Look at the picture. Complete sentences 1–4 with the words from the box.

| doctor | husband | son |
| friend | sister | teacher |

1 Bob: Tina is my wife. She's a doctor. This is my daughter, Poppy. And he is my _____, Connor.

2 Tina: Bob is my _____. He's a teacher in an English school.

3 Poppy: My mother is a _____ and my father is a _____. Connor is my big brother.

4 Connor: Poppy's my _____. She's eight. Kevin is my best _____. We're in the same class at school.

9 ▶6 Listen and check.

10 ▶7 Listen and repeat the words.

my **bro**ther	my **fa**ther	my **mo**ther	a **tea**cher
my **daugh**ter	my **friend**	my **sis**ter	my **wife**
a **doc**tor	my **hus**band	my **son**	

11 Write the names of five people in your life.

Macu   Hugh
Matthew   Rebeca
Shirley

12 Work in pairs. Give your names to your partner. Your partner asks questions.

A: *Who is Macu?*
B: *She's my wife.*
A: *Who is Matthew?*
B: *He's my friend.*

GRAMMAR

> **'m, 's, 're**
>
> **am**
> I**'m** Andrew.   (= I am)
>
> **is**
> She**'s** a doctor.   (= She is)
> He**'s** my brother.   (= He is)
> My name**'s** Ian   (= My name is)
> This **is** my friend, John.
>
> **are**
> You**'re** Naomi, right?   (= You are)
> We**'re** your teachers.   (= We are)
> They**'re** in my class.   (= They're)

13 Complete the sentences.

1 A: Who is Maria?
  B: She_____ my wife.

2 A: Who is he?
  B: Greg. He_____ our teacher.

3 A: Lara. This _____ my sister, Katia.
  B: Hi. Nice to meet you.

4 A: You_____ Ana, right?
  B: No. I_____ Zeynep. She_____ Ana!
  A: Oh! Sorry!

5 A: Who are they?
  B: _____'re my children!
  A: Nice! What are their names?
  B: My son is Cristiano and my daughter _____ Inés.

14 ▶8 Listen and check the answers.

15 ▶8 Listen again. Practise the conversations.

> **G** For more practice, see Exercises 1–4 on page 60.

CONVERSATION PRACTICE

16 Work in pairs. Say or ask who the people are. Choose 1 or 2:

1 Show photos on your phone.
2 Look at the photos in File 1 on page 80. They are your family and friends!

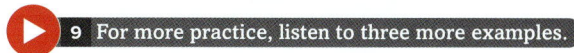

▶9 For more practice, listen to three more examples.

Unit 1   Be   9

WHERE'S THE PARTY?

REVIEW AND SPEAKING

1 Work in pairs. Say words for people.
son, friend ...

2 Work in pairs. Read the conversations. Use your own names.
A: *You're Khalid, right?*
B: *No. I'm Ben.*
A: *Oh, sorry.*

A: *You're Joan, right?*
B: *Yes – and you're Harry.*
A: *Yes. How are you?*
B: *Good, thanks.*

A: *Sorry. What's your name?*
B: *Ben. And you?*
A: *Tina. How are you?*
B: *Fine, thanks.*

3 Check the names of other people in the class.

VOCABULARY Numbers 13–22

4 ▶10 Listen and repeat the numbers.

13 thirteen	18 eighteen
14 fourteen	19 nineteen
15 fifteen	20 twenty
16 sixteen	21 twenty-one
17 seventeen	22 twenty-two

5 ▶11 Listen. Write the numbers.
1 _____, _____, _____, _____ [?]
2 _____, _____, _____, _____ [?]
3 _____, _____, _____, _____ [?]
4 _____, _____, _____, _____ [?]

6 Work in pairs. Look at Exercise 5 again. What's the next number?
A: *What's the number?*   A: *What's the number?*
B: *It's eighteen.*   B: *I don't know.*
A: *Yes, that's right.*

7 ▶12 Listen and check.

VOCABULARY Question words

8 ▶13 Look at the photos. Listen and repeat.

1 Where?

2 What time?

3 How old?

4 How long?

5 Who?

6 How much?

9 ▶14 Write the question words. Listen and check.
1 _____ is she? My wife.
2 _____ is it? São Paulo in Brazil.
3 _____ is it? Eight o'clock.
4 _____ is it? Twenty-two dollars.
5 _____ is it? Fifteen minutes.
6 _____ is she? She's thirteen.

10 ▶15 Listen to some questions and answers. Choose the answer you hear (a, b or c).
1 How are you?
  a Good.
  b Fine, thanks.
  c OK.
2 How long is the class?
  a One hour.
  b Three hours.
  c Twenty minutes.
3 How old are you?
  a Thirteen.
  b Eight.
  c Nineteen. I'm twenty on Saturday!
4 Where are you from?
  a New York.
  b China.
  c Here!
5 Who's she?
  a My mother.
  b That's my daughter.
  c My friend, Amani.
6 How much is lunch?
  a Fourteen euros.
  b Seven twenty.
  c Sixteen dollars.
7 What time is it?
  a Five.
  b Three o'clock.
  c Ten.
8 What's your phone number?
  a 71 33 68 922
  b 022 193 548
  c 069 455 781

V For more countries, see page 75.

10

GRAMMAR

Questions with *be*

are
A: How **are** you? | B: I'm OK.
A: Where **are** you from? | B: Japan.
A: **Are** you OK? | B: Yes, thanks.

is
A: How much **is** it? | B: Two pounds.
A: How old **is** he? | B: He's 18.
A: Who **is** she? | B: My teacher.
A: **Is** it nice? | B: Yes, it's good!

11 Complete the questions with *are* or *is*.
1 Where _____ you from?
2 How _____ you?
3 Where _____ he from?
4 How long _____ the class?
5 How old _____ you?
6 What time _____ the party?
7 How old _____ your son?
8 _____ she nice?
9 Who _____ he?
10 How much _____ it?

G For more practice, see Exercises 1–4 on page 61.

12 ▶16 Listen and check. The questions are fast then slow.

13 Work in pairs. Practise the questions.

SPEAKING

14 Write answers to the questions. Use one or two words.
- What time is it?
- How are you?
- Where are you from?
- How old are you?
- How long is the coffee break?

15 Work in pairs. Ask and answer the questions.

GRAMMAR

his, her, our, their
Tia**'s** party = **her** party
Pedro**'s** daughter = **his** daughter
Tom and Peter**'s** flat = **their** flat
Sara**'s** and my son = **our** son

G For practice, see Exercises 1 and 2 on pages 61 and 62.

READING

16 Read the invitations. Answer the questions.
1 What day is Tia's party?
2 What's Joe and Kate's phone number?
3 Where's Sara and Pedro's party?
4 Who is Santiago?
5 How long is Tom and Peter's party?
6 What number is Tom and Peter's flat?

17 Write five more questions about the parties.
1 How old is _____?
How old is Tia? / How old is Joe and Kate's daughter?
2 Where's _____?
3 What time is _____?
4 How long _____?
5 _____

18 Work in pairs. Ask and answer your questions from Exercise 17.

INVITATION!
OUR DAUGHTER TIA IS 18

Come to her party at:
Selale Restaurant
25 Green Lanes
Friday 15th
9pm – 2am

Joe and Kate's phone: 121 786 5539

SARA AND PEDRO
HAVE A NEW BABY BOY!

Come to our party and meet Santiago
(and his sister Rebeca!)

The Spanish Centre | Saturday 16th
3 High Street | 12pm – 6pm
| Lunch at 2pm

Mobile: 07311 762 4683

TOM AND PETER HAVE A NEW FLAT

COME TO OUR PARTY AT
Flat 6 Floor 3
19 Old Street

3pm – 8pm
This Sunday (17th)
email: tom@xmail.com

Unit 1 Be

TIME FOR COFFEE

Coffee and cake

VOCABULARY Times and prices

1 ▶18 Listen and repeat the numbers.

20	twenty	60	sixty
21	twenty-one	65	sixty-five
30	thirty	70	seventy
32	thirty-two	76	seventy-six
40	forty	80	eighty
43	forty-three	87	eighty-seven
50	fifty	90	ninety
54	fifty-four	98	ninety-eight

Times
10.25 ten twenty five
2.00   two   two o'clock
16.30 four thirty   sixteen thirty

Prices
£3.99   three ninety-nine   three pounds ninety-nine
€17.50 seventeen fifty   seventeen euros fifty

2 ▶19 Listen. Write the time or price.

1 It's 3._____.
2 It's £15._____.
3 The class is at _____.
4 The coffee break is at _____.
5 A cappuccino is €_____.
6 Lunch is at _____.
7 Sandwiches are $_____.
8 My bus is at _____.

3 Work in pairs. Remember the questions from Exercise 2. Ask and answer the questions.

VOCABULARY In a coffee shop

4 ▶20 Listen and repeat words from a menu.

americano	espresso	medium	small
cake	large	orange juice	tea
cappuccino	latte	sandwich	water

5 ▶21 Listen and repeat the words in sentences.

6 Work in pairs. Ask the prices. Complete the menu.

Student A: look at the menu on this page.
Student B: look at the menu in File 2 on page 81.
A: *How much is a medium cappuccino?*

MENU

	Large	Medium	Small
Hot drinks			
cappuccino	3.75	_____	2.90
latte	_____	3.40	_____
americano	_____	2.80	2.30
espresso	2.05	1.60	
tea	2.25	1.95	1.60
Cold drinks			
fresh orange juice	_____	3.95	3.45
Coke	2.15		
water		_____	
Food			
cakes 4.95	sandwiches _____		

7 Ask about prices.
How much is a cappuccino in your country?
How much is _____ in _____?

12

DEVELOPING CONVERSATIONS

Ordering and serving drinks
A: *What would you like?*
B: *A large americano.*
A: *Americano.* **Anything else?**
B: *Yes – one medium orange juice.*
A: *OK. Anything else?*
B: **No, thanks.**
A: *OK. That's £7.05 (seven oh five).*

8 ▶22 Listen to the conversation.

9 Have similar conversations. Use the menu on page 12.

LISTENING

10 ▶23 Listen to a man in a coffee shop. Tick (✓) the food and drink on the menu. How much is it?

11 ▶24 Listen to part 2 of the conversation. What's the problem (a, b or c)?
   a It's not the right coffee.
   b It's not the right money.
   c It's not a large cappuccino.

GRAMMAR

not
It's **not** right.
It's **not** a black tea.
It's **not** fifty pounds.
It's medium – **not** large.
My tea – it's **not** hot!

12 Add *not*.
   1 A: What's the problem?
      B: My tea – it's ⌃not right.
   2 A: What's the problem?
      B: My coffee – it's a cappuccino.
   3 A: Yes, sir. Are you OK?
      B: Sorry. It's a small tea – large.
   4 A: Are you OK?
      B: No. It's coffee cake – chocolate.
   5 A: Is everything OK?
      B: No. My tea's hot.
   6 A: What's the problem?
      B: It's right. It's 35 euros. It's 29.

13 ▶25 Listen and check.

14 ▶26 Listen and repeat the answers.

15 Have similar conversations. Use the pictures.

1

A: *What's the problem?*　　A: *Are you OK?*
B: *My coffee, it's small –*　B: *It's not a large coffee.*
　not large.　　　　　　　A: *Sorry.*
A: *Sorry.*

2 　　**3**

4 　　**5**

Ⓖ For more practice, see Exercise 1 on page 62.

SPEAKING

16 Have conversations. Take turns.

Student A: assistant	**Student B:** customer
Hi. How are you?	
What would you like?	
Anything else?	
That's	
	Here you are.
Are you OK?	
	No, ...
Oh, yes. Sorry. Here you are.	
	Thanks.

PRONUNCIATION AND REVIEW

17 ▶27 Listen to the sentences. They are fast. Write the number.

This is my son, John.	___
This is my friend, Don.	___
Where are you from?	___
What's her name?	_1_
What time is the class?	___
What's your phone number?	___

18 ▶28 Listen and check the answers. They are slow then fast.

19 Work in pairs. Say the sentences. Reply.
   A: *This is my son, John.*　B: *Hello. Nice to meet you.*

Ⓖ For more pronunciation, see Exercise 1 on page 62.

Unit 1　Be　13

2 LIVE, WORK, EAT

IN THIS UNIT YOU LEARN HOW TO:

- ask and say where you live
- ask about someone's job
- talk about people you know
- understand a menu
- say what you like / don't like
- answer a waiter and order food

WORDS FOR UNIT 2

1 Look at the words and photos.

1 a big **ci**ty	7 some **meat**
2 **near** and **far**	8 a **ta**xi **dri**ver
3 a lot of **chil**dren	9 fresh **fruit**
4 it's ex**pen**sive	10 **work** in an **o**ffice
5 some **nur**ses	11 **walk** in the **park**
6 I don't **like** it	12 a small **vi**llage

2 ▶ 29 Listen and repeat the words.

3 Work in pairs. Don't look at the words.

Student A: say the number.

Student B: say the word(s).

Unit 2   Live, work, eat   15

WHERE DO YOU LIVE?

LISTENING AND SPEAKING

1. ▶ 30 Listen to Freya and Adam.

   F: Hi, you're Adam, right?
   A: Yes. Sorry. What's your name?
   F: Freya.
   A: Oh yes. How are you?
   F: Good. And you?
   A: Yeah, I'm OK.
   F: Where do you live?
   A: Kings Heath. And you?
   F: I live on New Road. Do you know it?
   A: No. Is it near here?
   F: Yes. I walk here. It takes ten minutes.

2. ▶ 31 Listen and repeat.

   1 **Where** do you **live**?
   2 Do you **know** it?
   3 Is it **near here**?
   4 It takes **ten mi**nutes.

3. Work in pairs. Practise the conversation from Exercise 1. Change the words in red.

VOCABULARY My home

4. Write the words in the box with the correct photo.

a city   flats   the north   a road   a village

5. ▶ 32 Listen and repeat.

a **vi**llage	a **road**	the **north**
a **ci**ty	a **house**	the **south**
an **a**rea	**flats**	the **cen**tre

6. ▶ 33 Listen to Leo. Choose the correct word(s).

   My name's Leo.
   I'm from [1] *Chile / Argentina*.
   I live in a [2] *village / city* called Temuco.
   Temuco **is in an area called** Araucanía.
   It's in the [3] *north / south* **of** Chile.
   I live in a small [4] *house / flat* with my
   [5] *son / daughter* and [6] *my wife / my dog*.
   It's on Los Leones **road**.
   It's near [7] *a big park / the university*.

7. Make the sentences from Exercise 6 true for you. Tell a partner.

   My name's ...
   I'm from ...

GRAMMAR

Present simple

I	**live** near here.
You	**know** the city.
We	**like** Rio.
They	**walk** to the centre.
My mother and father	**have** a nice house.
He	**lives** near here.
She	**knows** the city.
My brother	**likes** Rio.
My friend Karen	**has** a nice flat.
It	**takes** ten minutes.

8 Tell the class about your partner.

His name's Leo.
He's from Chile.
He lives in a city ...

> For more practice, see Exercise 1 on page 62.

9 Write three sentences about friends and family. Use the verbs in the Grammar box or a dictionary.

*My mother **lives** with me.*
*My friend Fei **has** a Ferrari.*
*My sister **knows** our teacher. They**'re** friends.*

10 Work in pairs. Say your sentences.

GRAMMAR

Present simple questions: *do you*

Where **do you** live?
Who **do you** live with?
Do you live near here?
Do you know it?

11 Put the words in the correct order. Make questions.

1 live / where / do / you / ?
2 with your brother / do / live / you / ?
3 who / you / live / with / do / ?
4 do / your / city / you / like / ?
5 you / know / my / name / do / ?
6 do / a / you / have / house / or / flat / a / ?

12 ▶ 34 Listen and check the questions.

13 ▶ 35 Listen and repeat the questions.

14 Work in pairs. Ask and answer the questions.

> For more practice, see Exercises 1–4 on page 63.

DEVELOPING CONVERSATIONS

And you?

We use *And you?* to ask the same 'you-question'.
A: *How are you?*
B: *Good, thanks. **And you?*** (= How are *you*?)
A: *I'm OK.*
A: *Do you like Tokyo?*
B: *Yes, it's great! **And you?*** (= Do *you* like Tokyo?)
A: *No, I don't like it. It's very big.*

15 Work in pairs. Take turns.

Student A: ask questions 1–6.

Student B: answer and ask *And you?*

Student A: answer.

1 How are you?
2 What's your name?
3 Where do you live?
4 How old are you?
5 Do you have any brothers or sisters?
6 Do you like grammar?

CONVERSATION PRACTICE

16 Complete the conversation.

and	it	live	~~name~~	to	takes
do	know	meet	on	you (x3)	~~your~~

A: Hi. Sorry, what's ¹___*your*___ ___*name*___?
B: Ali. And you?
A: Maria. Nice ²_____ _____ you.
B: You too.
A: So, Ali. Where ³_____ _____ live?
B: Clayton. It's a small village. Do you know it?
A: No. Is it far?
B: It takes thirty minutes by car. ⁴_____ _____? Where do you live?
A: I ⁵_____ _____ Havana Road. Do ⁶_____ _____ it?
B: Yes. It's near here, right?
A: Yes. I walk here. ⁷_____ _____ fifteen minutes.

17 ▶ 36 Listen and check.

18 Have similar conversations. Talk to other people in the class. Find someone who:

• lives near you.
• lives far from you.

 37 For more practice, listen to another example.

Unit 2 Live, work, eat

WHAT DO YOU DO?

REVIEW AND SPEAKING

1 Choose one or two:
   - Look at the photos on pages 14 and 15. Test each other.
   - Study the conversation in Exercise 1, page 16. Close your book and practise the conversation.
   - Ask other students *Who do you live with?*

VOCABULARY Jobs

2 ▶ 38 Listen and repeat the words.

| a **bus driver** | a **nurse** | a **student** | a **wai**ter |
| a **mum** | retired | a **tea**cher | **work** in an **office** |

3 ▶ 39 Listen to eight conversations. What do they do? Write the letter of the photo.

1 ___a___   4 _____   7 _____
2 _____   5 _____   8 _____
3 _____   6 _____

4 Work in pairs. Practise conversations. Student B close your book. Take turns.

Student A: ask *What do you do?*

Student B: say *I'm … / I work in …*

Student A: point to the correct photo.

SPEAKING

5 Work in groups. What jobs do people you know do? Use the jobs from Exercise 2.

My friend James is a …
My brother works …
My mother ….

6 Say which jobs are:
   a great.   b good.   c OK.

GRAMMAR

Present simple: *don't (do not)*

I **work** 50 hours a week.	I **don't work**. I'm retired.
I **walk** to school.	I **don't walk** to school.
You **like** the job.	You **don't like** the job.
We **have** a flat.	We **don't have** a flat.
They **have** a lot of money.	They **don't have** a lot of money.

a

b

c

d

e

f

g

h

7 Make the sentences negative.
1. I work on Friday and Saturday.
2. I know.
3. You live near here.
4. I like it.
5. We have children.
6. They live in the centre.
7. I walk to class.
8. I go to a language school.

8 ▶ 40 Listen and repeat the negative sentences from Exercise 7.

G For more practice, see Exercises 1 and 2 on page 63.

9 Complete the sentences. Make them true for you. Use these verbs or others.

| go | know | live | work | have | like | walk |

- I don't _____
- I don't _____
- I don't _____
- I'm not _____

10 Tell a partner your sentences.

READING

11 Read about four people's jobs. Answer the questions.
1. Where are the four people from?
2. Which city do they all live in?

12 Read again. Write the names of the people.
1. I'm a taxi driver. _____
2. I'm a nurse. _____
3. I'm a teacher. _____
4. I'm a student. _____
5. I like my job. _____ and _____
6. I live near my job. _____
7. I work a lot of hours. _____

13 ▶ 42 Listen to Carlos and read again. <u>Underline</u> two things that are different.

14 ▶ 43 Listen to the three other people and read again. Underline the two things that are different for each person.

GRAMMAR

Plural / no plural

Singular	Plural	No plural
a doctor	The doctor**s** **are** nice.	The money **is** good.
a job	I have three job**s**.	I don't have time.
an hour	The hour**s** **are** good.	I have some money.
a person	The people **are** nice.	I have a lot of work.
a child	I have two children.	

G For practice, see Exercises 1–3 on page 64.

15 ▶ 44 Listen to the conversation. Who is it?

16 Work in pairs. Have similar conversations. Take turns. Who is it?

Student A: ask the questions *What do you do? Do you like it? Why? / Why not?*

Student B: answer the questions. You are Ali, Jessica, Rasa or Carlos.

WRITING AND SPEAKING

17 Change the words in red so the sentences are true for you. Use a dictionary to help you.

I'm a teacher. I work in a university. I like my job. The hours are good. The people are nice. The money's good.

18 Ask other people in the class the questions from Exercise 16 about their real jobs.

THE WORLD IN ONE CITY

▶ 41

My name's Carlos. I'm from Mexico, but now I live in London. I live in north London and I work in a university in the centre. It takes thirty minutes by train. The job's great. I like my students and the money's OK.

My name's Jessica. I'm from Australia, but I'm a nurse here in London. My job's OK, but I don't like the hospital. It's big and I don't live near it. It's an hour by car from my house. The other nurses are nice, but I don't like some doctors.

My name's Rasa. I'm from Lithuania, but now I live and work in Tooting – an area in south London. I work in a coffee shop. It's OK. I like the people and the hours are good for me. I work from nine to three and then I go to university.

My name's Ali. I'm from Turkey. I work for a taxi company. I don't like my job. London traffic is bad. The money is bad and I work a lot – 70 or 80 hours a week. I don't have time with my wife and two children.

Unit 2 Live, work, eat

TABLE FOR TWO

VOCABULARY Food and drinks

1 ▶ 45 Listen and repeat.

chicken	fish	ice cream	meat	salad
drinks	fruit	juice	rice	

2 Complete the menu on page 21 with the words from Exercise 1.

GRAMMAR

3 ▶ 46 Work in groups. Listen to the example.

A: I love meat.
B: I don't like it. I only eat fish or vegetables.
C: I like chicken, but I don't like bacon.
A: I love chips.
B: Me too! I love chips.
C: I don't like them.

4 Say the food and drinks you love / like / don't like. Find one thing you all:
- love.
- don't like.

G For more practice, see Exercise 1 on page 64.

SPEAKING

5 Work in pairs. Look at the words in the box. Then read the examples.

A: *Fruit juice?*
B: *Three euros 50.*
A: *OK.*

A: *Beef burger?*
B: *Fourteen euros.*
A: *No. **Less**.*
B: *Twelve euros.*

A: *Salmon?*
B: *Ten euros.*
A: *No. **More**.*

6 It's your restaurant. Decide the prices. Have similar conversations to the examples in Exercise 5. Write the prices for each dish on page 21.

7 Change partner. Ask about prices. Say *It's expensive*, *It's OK* or *It's cheap*.

A: *How much is your kebab?*
B: *Sixteen euros.*
A: *Oh. It's expensive.*
B: *Our kebab is good. Very nice!*

LISTENING

8 ▶ 47 Listen to a waiter and family. Tick (✓) the drinks the family orders on the menu.

9 ▶ 48 Listen. Tick (✓) the food they order.

10 ▶ 49 Listen. Complete the conversation with one word in each space.

A: Do you have a table for ¹_____?
B: Yes. Would you like a menu in ²_____?
A: Please.
B: Would you like some drinks?
A: Yes. Two orange juices, a Coke and ³_____ water.
...
B: Are you ready to order?
A: Yes. A kebab with rice for ⁴_____.
B: OK. And for ⁵_____?
C: Chicken, please.
B: With ⁶_____ or chips?
C: Chips, please.
B: And you?
D: Prawns with rice.
B: Anything ⁷_____? A salad?
C: How much is the tomato salad?
B: ⁸_____ euros.
C: Oh. It's expensive. No, ⁹_____.
B: So, that's one kebab and rice, one chicken and chips, and one prawns with rice.

DEVELOPING CONVERSATIONS

Ordering food
*A Coke and some water, **please**.*
*Chicken **for me** and a kebab for my son.*

11 Work in threes. One person is the waiter. Ask and answer the questions.
- Would you like some drinks?
- Are you ready to order?
- What would you like?
- And you?

20

SPEAKING

12 Work in pairs. One person is the waiter. Practise the conversation. Change the information in red.

A: *Do you have a table for four?*
B: *Yes. Would you like a menu in English?*
A: *Please.*
B: *Would you like some drinks?*
A: *Yes, please. One coffee, two orange juices.*

13 Work in groups of four. Close your books. Practise similar conversations to the one in Exercise 10. Choose your food and drink.

PRONUNCIATION AND REVIEW

14 ▶ 50 Listen to the sentences below. They are fast. Write the number.

Where do you live?	_____	They have a nice house.	_____
I don't know it.	_____	It's in the north.	_____
I don't live near here.	_____	He's a student at university.	_____
I like it here.	_____	I don't like it.	_____
It's a nice area.	1	She's a teacher in a language school.	_____

15 ▶ 51 Listen and check the answers. They are slow then fast.

16 Practise saying the sentences.

17 Work in pairs. In one minute:
- write words for jobs and work.
- write words for food.

Ⓖ For more pronunciation, see Exercises 1 and 2 on page 64.

1 _____

burger
kebab
2 _____ curry
grilled chicken
hot bacon sandwich

MENU

3 _____ AND
SEAFOOD

cod

salmon

prawns

SIDE DISHES

bread   green 5 _____
chips   tomato salad
4 _____ vegetables

VEGETARIAN DISHES

cheese pizza   vegetable curry

DESSERTS

6 _____ (vanilla, chocolate, strawberry)
chocolate or carrot cake
fresh 7 _____

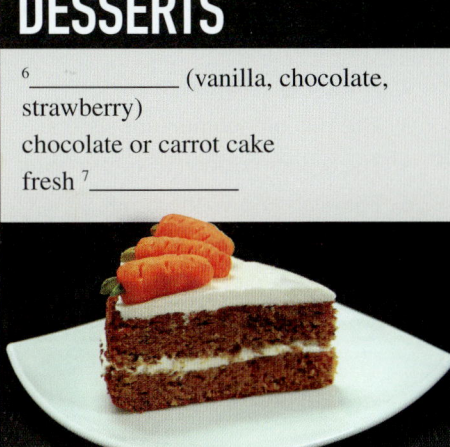

8 _____
water
coffee
Coke
tea
fresh orange 9 _____

Unit 2 Live, work, eat   21

VIDEO 1

PEOPLE

1 Look at the photo. Where are the people from? Use the words on page 75 to help you.

2 ▶1 Watch the video. Number the sentences when you hear them.
   a This is us. People. Nice to meet you.   6
   b This is us. Lots of people from different countries.   1
   c We meet as a family. We talk.   2
   d We meet on the train. We talk.   4
   e We meet in the street. We talk.   3
   f We are friends. We do the same things.   2

3 Are the sentences true (T) or false (F)?
   1 The baby is a boy. F
   2 The baby is two years old. F
   3 The two old women are sisters. F
   4 The woman doesn't like the book. F
   5 The man knows the book. T
   6 The women want a coffee. T
   7 The boy is nine. F

4 ▶1 Watch the video again and check.

5 Complete the sentences with one word in each space.
   1 We are friends. _____ do the same things.
   2 _____'s a boy. _____ name's Josh.
   3 Her daughter _____ a son. _____'s two.
   4 The book. Do you like _____?
   5 Would _____ like a break?
   6 You'_____ ten!

6 Work in groups. Answer the questions.
   • Do you have any friends from another country? Where are they from?
   • What times do you have a break in the day? How long are your breaks?

SPEAKING

7 Work in pairs. Ask and answer questions about people. Use the photos on page 18 or page 80 or photos of people on your phone. Change the words in red.

Who's she?	My sister.
What's her name?	Juana.
What does she do?	She's a nurse.
How old is she?	23.
Where does she live?	Mexico City. She lives with me.

REVIEW 1

GRAMMAR

1 Choose the correct word(s).
1 How old *is / are* you?
2 What *is / are* her name?
3 Where *are you / you are / do you* live?
4 She *has / have* a new car.
5 We have three *childs / children* – two *son / sons* and a daughter.
6 Do you know Andrew? This is *his / their / our* wife.
7 Who *are / do / is* you live with?
8 Where *is / are / do* they from?
9 We *not / don't / are not* live here.
10 *I'm not / I don't / I not* like meat.

2 Rewrite the sentences as negatives (–) or questions (?).
1 It's expensive. (–)
2 His mother is retired. (?)
3 They have a lot of money. (–)
4 You work near here. (?)
5 I have a sister. (–)
6 The teachers are nice. (?)
7 I know her brother. (–)
8 He likes English. (?)

3 Complete the sentences with one word in each space. Contractions (*I'm*, *don't*, etc.) are one word.
1 I like tea, but I _____ like coffee.
2 It's my husband's birthday on Saturday. Come to _____ party.
3 I walk to university. I _____ have a car.
4 Excuse me. This is _____ a cappuccino. It's a latte.
5 I like my job. The hours _____ OK and the money _____ very good.
6 It's not far. It _____ ten minutes by car.
7 I don't have time today. I have a _____ of work.
8 Where _____ you live? _____ it near here?

4 Write full questions to complete the conversation. Use the words in brackets.
A: ¹_____? (name)
B: Isabella.
A: And ²_____? (from)
B: Cuzco. In Peru.
A: ³_____? (old)
B: Twenty-seven.
A: ⁴_____? (do)
B: I'm a doctor. I work in a hospital in the city centre.
A: ⁵_____? (job)
B: Yes, I do. I love it. I like the people and the money is OK.

VOCABULARY

5 Match the verbs in the box with the correct groups of words (1–7).

have	know	like	live	take	walk	work

1 _____ in an office / forty hours a week
2 _____ ten minutes / twenty minutes by train
3 _____ in a village / near here
4 _____ a big house / children
5 _____ in the park / to school
6 _____ my job / fish and chips
7 _____ your name / the area

6 Put the words into three groups: food, drinks or jobs.

americano	fish	salad	teacher
chicken	nurse	sandwich	waiter
Coke	orange juice	taxi driver	water
doctor	rice	tea	

7 Replace the words in italics with their opposites from the box.

brother	daughter	small	wife
cheap	father	south	

1 This is my *husband*.
   This is my wife.
2 This is my *sister*.
3 This is my *mother*.
4 This is my *son*.
5 It's in the *north*.
6 It's very *expensive*.
7 It's a *big* town.

8 Complete the text with the words from the box.

brother	flat	nice	park
city	name	north	student

My ¹_____ is Maryam and I'm a ²_____. I'm from Oman. I live in a small ³_____ called Khasab. It's in the ⁴_____ of Oman. I live in a big ⁵_____ with my mother, father and ⁶_____. We live near a ⁷_____. It's very ⁸_____.

9 Match the questions (1–8) with the answers (a–h).
1 Who's he?   a Twenty-three.
2 Where do you live?   b Ninety minutes.
3 How long is the class?   c 07781-336-454
4 What time is it?   d My father.
5 How old is she?   e Two euros twenty.
6 What day is the party?   f Eight thirty.
7 How much is it?   g In Rome.
8 What's your phone number?   h Friday.

Review 1   23

3 LOVE, WANT, NEED

IN THIS UNIT YOU LEARN HOW TO:

- ask how things are
- respond to good and bad news
- use adjectives to describe things
- ask and talk about things people have
- ask someone to repeat

WORDS FOR UNIT 3

1 Look at the words and photos.

1 a ho**tel room**	7 go on **hol**iday
2 he **needs** a **show**er	8 get mar**ried**
3 **read** a **book**	9 old **shoes**
4 buy **clothes**	10 very **hot**
5 **wea**ther	11 he's not **well**
6 a **show**er	12 take the **train** to **work**

2 ▶ 52 Listen and repeat the words.

3 Work in pairs. Don't look at the words.

Student A: say the number.

Student B: say the word(s).

Unit 3 Love, want, need 25

a

b

c

d

HOW IS IT?

SPEAKING

1 ▶ 53 Listen to two conversations.

1
A: Hi. How are you?
B: Good, thanks. And you?
A: Yeah – not bad!

2
A: Hi. How are you?
B: Very good. And you?
A: I'm not very well.
B: Oh, I'm sorry.

2 Work in pairs. Practise the conversations from Exercise 1.

3 Ask other students in the class *How are you?*

VOCABULARY Adjectives

4 ▶ 54 Listen and repeat the adjectives. Tick (✓) the words you know.

bad	expensive	hungry	old
big	good	married	small
cold	great	new	tired
difficult	hot	nice	well

5 Say two or three adjectives for each photo.

6 Don't look at the adjectives in Exercise 4.
1) Complete sentences 1–6 with an adjective.
2) Complete the sentences with a different adjective.

1 It's **a/an** _____ **flat.**
2 It's **a/an** _____ **class.**
3 It's **a/an** _____ **hotel.**
4 It's _____ **weather.**
5 They're _____ **clothes.**
6 I'm _____.

---

a / an
a nice flat   **an o**ld flat
a big hotel   **an e**xpensive hotel

---

7 Compare your answers.

8 Write the correct numbers.

| −15°C | 98 | 78 | 0°C |

1 It's cold. _____
2 It's very cold. _____
3 He's old. _____
4 She's very old. _____

9 Work in groups. Say things you love / like / don't like.

   A: *I love very hot weather.*
   B: *Me too.*
   C: *I don't like very hot weather.*
   A: *I like big cities.*
   B: *I don't like them. I like small cities.*
   C: *Me too.*

LISTENING

10 Where are the people? Match the questions (1–4) with the places (a–d).

   1 How's the class?   a in a hotel
   2 How's the chicken?   b in a restaurant
   3 How's your room?   c in a school
   4 How's the weather?   d on holiday / in a different country

11 ▶ 55 Listen. What question from Exercise 10 do they ask in each conversation?

   Conversation 1: _____
   Conversation 2: _____
   Conversation 3: _____
   Conversation 4: _____

12 ▶ 55 Listen again. Choose the correct word(s).

   1 A: It's *not very* / *very* big.
     B: The same. And it's *cold* / *old*!
   2 English is *difficult* / *good*.
   3 A: How's the fish?
     B: It's *great* / *not very nice*.
   4 A: It's *cold* / *hot*.
     B: Oh no! It's normally *near* / *hot* there.

GRAMMAR

Negatives with *be*

'm not
I**'m not** well.

're not
We**'re not** tired.
They**'re not** in my class.
You**'re not** English, right?

's not
He**'s not** married.
She**'s not** here.
It**'s not** very difficult.

13 Make the sentences negative.

   1 She's my friend.   5 They're from here.
   2 It's a big city.   6 The rooms are very expensive.
   3 We're married.   7 My job's very good. The money's great.
   4 I'm very hungry.

14 ▶ 56 Listen and check. The sentences are fast then slow.

15 Work in pairs. Practise the sentences.

16 Work in pairs. Say true sentences about you and where you live.

   I'm not married.
   My flat's not very big.
   Moscow is very expensive.

   G For more practice, see Exercises 1 and 2 on page 65.

DEVELOPING CONVERSATIONS

Responding to news

For good news
A: *The teacher's nice.*
B: **Oh, good.**

For bad news
A: *I'm not very well.*
B: **I'm sorry.**

17 ▶ 57 Listen and repeat the phrases from the box.

18 Write *Oh, good* or *I'm sorry* after each sentence.

   1 It's not very expensive. _____
   2 My room is nice and big. _____
   3 It's very cold in my flat. _____
   4 The weather here is great. _____
   5 I love my English class. _____
   6 The fish is very good. _____
   7 My father's not very well. _____
   8 I don't like my new job. The hours are very bad. _____

19 ▶ 58 Listen and answer.

20 Work in pairs. Take turns.

   Student A: say a sentence from Exercise 18.
   Student B: say *Oh, good* or *I'm sorry*.

CONVERSATION PRACTICE

21 Write questions starting with *How's ... ?*

   1 in a hotel   4 in a different country
   2 in a restaurant   5 about a new flat/house
   3 at school

22 Have your own conversations.

Unit 3 Love, want, need 27

THINGS I WANT IN LIFE

REVIEW

1 Choose two:
- Write or say all the adjectives you know.
- Add eight different words to *I'm ...*
  I'm cold.
  I'm 16.
- Say five things about you and your things with *not*.
  I don't live near here.
  My flat is not expensive.

VOCABULARY *go, take, want*

2 Look at the sentences. Then match the verbs in the box with the groups of words 1–3.
- He / She takes the train to work.
- He / She wants a new car.
- He / She goes to the gym every day.

go	take	want

1 _____ the bus
a photo
a shower
a long time

2 _____ to the park every day
to the doctor
on holiday
shopping

3 _____ a coffee
a new house
to go to China
to buy some clothes

3 ▶60 Listen to the phrases and repeat them.

4 Work in pairs. Take turns.

Student A: say a verb. *go*

Student B: don't look. Say a phrase. *go shopping*

GRAMMAR

Present simple: *doesn't*

wants	→	She **doesn't want** to go.
takes	→	It **doesn't take** a long time.
likes	→	He **doesn't like** coffee
goes	→	The bus **doesn't go** to the centre.

5 Complete the sentences with the verbs.
1 My sister ___has___ two children. (have)
2 He _____ lots of money. (not have)
3 The number 30 bus _____ near my house. (go)
4 He _____ to university. (not go)
5 He _____ his job. (like)
6 My mother _____ big cities. (not like)
7 My dad _____ the bus to work. He walks. (not take)
8 My friend, Marc, _____ for Google. He _____ in San Francisco. (work / live)

6 Make six negative sentences about people you know. Use these verbs.

go	have	live	take	want	work

7 Work in pairs. Say your sentences.

G For more practice, see Exercise 1 on page 65.

WHAT DO PEOPLE WANT?

HERE ARE FIVE THINGS PEOPLE SAY THEY WANT.
1. I want to be happy.
2. I want to be well and live a long life.
3. I want more free time.
4. I want more money.
5. I want a good job.

▶ 61

JOSH
I want a new mobile phone for my birthday. My phone is very old! I want some money to go shopping too. My mum buys my clothes, but I don't like them. They're for old people!

BETTINA
I have a good job. I love my husband. We have a big house and a nice car. We go on holiday to nice places. It's all great, but we don't have children and now we want a family.

MATTHIEU
I only work for two days a week – fifteen or twenty hours. I don't have a lot of money, but I don't want a lot of things. Money's not important to me. I have food. I only drink water. I have friends. I have some books to read. I have a lot of free time.

ANGELO
I'm a teacher. I live in the city, but I work in a village. I go by car and it takes me two hours. At the end of the day, I'm very tired. I want a job in the city. I want to walk to work and have more free time. But it's difficult.

READING

8 Read five things people want. Tick (✓) the things *you* want.

9 Read about the four people. Answer the questions.
1. What does Josh want for his birthday?
2. Does Josh like his clothes?
3. Is Bettina married?
4. Does Bettina have a daughter?
5. Does Matthieu work a lot?
6. Does Matthieu want more money?
7. What does Angelo do?
8. How long does it take Angelo to get to work?

GRAMMAR

Present simple questions: *does*
What **does he** do?
Why **does she** want a new job?
How long **does it** take to get to work?

10 Complete the questions with the name of people in the class. Use a different name in each sentence.
- What does _____ do?
- Does _____ have any brothers or sisters?
- Where does _____ live?
- Where does _____ work?
- How does _____ come to class?
- What food does _____ like?

11 Work in groups. Ask and answer the questions about people in the class.
A: *What does X do?*
B: *I don't know.*
C: *She's a teacher.*

 For more practice, see Exercises 1 and 2 on page 65.

WRITING

12 Write four sentences about things you have and things you want – and don't want – in your life. Say why. Use a dictionary if you need to.

Unit 3 Love, want, need 29

DO YOU NEED ANYTHING?

my mobile   **a** map   **a** pen   **a** towel

a dictionary   **a** brush   **a** char**ger**   **a small** bag

a big coat   **lots of** clothes   soap   **some** cash

some**thing to** read   food **from** home   **some other** shoes   **a** tooth**brush and** tooth**paste**

VOCABULARY Things

1 What do you need on holiday? Tick (✓) the things you take with you.

2 ▶ 62 Listen and repeat the words from Exercise 1.

3 Work in pairs. Say what you take on holiday. Think about these times and places.
- a weekend in a city
- a week to visit friends or family
- two weeks in a hotel in a hot country

LISTENING

4 ▶ 63 Listen. Answer the questions.
1 Who are the people in the picture? Write the names.
2 Where is Wilton from?

5 ▶ 64 Listen to Part 2. Answer the questions.
1 How long does it take from Peru to the UK?
2 Is Wilton tired?
3 What food or drink does Wilton want?
4 What else does he need?

DEVELOPING CONVERSATIONS

Asking for help in conversation

When you don't hear a word
Sorry? **Can you say that again?**

When you don't know a word
How do you say batería *(in English)?*

6 ▶ 65 Listen to a conversation.
1 What's the woman's question?
2 What's the man's answer?

7 ▶66 Listen. Then work in pairs. Practise the questions in the box. Use your own words.

8 Listen to the questions your teacher asks. Use the phrases from the box.

T: *What do you do?*
S: *Sorry, can you say that again?*
T: *Do you have a towel?*
S: *Sorry, can you say that again?*

9 Ask other students in your class. *How do you say [English word] in your language?* Use words from Exercise 1. Do the words sound the same or very different?

10 Work in groups. Think of three more things you take on holiday.

GRAMMAR

a and any

Do you have Do you need Do you want	a	towel? pen?
	any	towels? other clothes? money? toothpaste?
	anything (else)?	
I don't have I don't need I don't want	a	charger.
	any	other clothes. milk.
	anything (else).	

11 Say things from Exercise 1 you *don't* take on holiday. Why?

I don't take any towels on holiday. The hotel has towels.
I don't take a dictionary. I have one on my phone!

12 Complete the sentences with *a* or *any*.

1 A: Do you need _____ dictionary?
   B: No, thanks. I understand the word.
2 A: Do you have _____ money? I only have euros.
   B: Yes. How much do you need?
3 A: It's very cold here. Do you have _____ other clothes?
   B: Yes. I have a big coat.
4 A: Do you need _____ towel?
   B: No, it's OK. I have one.
5 A: Do you want _____ food?
   B: Yes, please. I'm hungry.
6 A: Do you have _____ brothers or sisters?
   B: Yes. One brother and three sisters.

13 ▶67 Listen and check.

14 Work in groups. Ask and answer six questions with *Do you have/want/need …*. Use words from Exercise 1.

G For more practice, see Exercise 1 on page 66.

SPEAKING

15 **Student A:** you are a student like Wilton. Write three questions on paper to ask your host.

Do you have a towel?

Student B: you are a host like Janet. Write three questions on paper to ask your student.

Do you want to have a shower?

16 Give your questions to your partner. Write answers to your partner's questions.

A: *Do you have a towel?*
B: *Of course. Wait here.*
A: *Do you need to have a shower?*
B: *No. I'm OK now. Later.*

17 Have conversations. Use your questions and answers.

A: *Hello. Are you …?*
B: *Yes.*
A: *Hi. Nice to meet you! I'm ….*
B: *Hello …. Nice to meet you, too.*
A: *Come in. Leave your bag there.*
B: *OK.*
A: *…*

PRONUNCIATION AND REVIEW

18 ▶68 Listen to the sentences. They are fast. Write the number.

How's the weather?	___
How's your class?	___
It's not very expensive.	___
It's not very nice. It's very cold.	___
Do you have any brothers or sisters?	___
Do you have a pen?	*1*
Do you want to go shopping?	___
I don't have a lot of free time.	___

19 ▶69 Listen and check the answers. They are slow then fast.

20 Practise saying the sentences.

21 Work in pairs. In one minute, say:
  • adjectives
  • things you have

G For more pronunciation, see Exercises 1 and 2 on page 66.

Unit 3 Love, want, need 31

4 WHERE AND WHEN?

IN THIS UNIT YOU LEARN HOW TO:
- ask about places and say what's there
- understand simple directions
- talk about your week
- ask for help / ask to do things in class

WORDS FOR UNIT 4

1 Look at the words and photos.

1 a **walk** on the **beach**	7 in the **train sta**tion
2 **turn off** your **phone**	8 it's **not o**pen
3 **get up early**	9 **first** (1st), **se**cond (2nd) and **third** (3rd)
4 **see** a **film**	10 how **many**?
5 **left** and **right**	11 **cash ma**chines
6 sit **next** to the **pool**	12 a **church** at **night**

2 ▶70 Listen and repeat the words.

3 Work in pairs. Don't look at the words.

Student A: say the number.

Student B: say the words.

Unit 4 Where and when? 33

the city of São Paulo in Brazil

a village called Agüero in Spain

a town called Ludlow in the UK

IS THERE A BANK NEAR HERE?

VOCABULARY Places

1. Look at the three photos of places. Which places do you like / don't you like? Are they good places to live / go for a holiday?

2. Tick (✓) the words you know. Compare in pairs.

a **b**ank	a **c**inema	a **p**ark
a **c**afé	a **c**lothes shop	a **res**taurant
a **c**ar park	a **hos**pital	a **s**upermarket
a **c**ash ma**chine**	a **h**otel	a **sw**imming pool
a **church**	a **m**arket	the **t**rain sta**tion**

3. ▶ 71 Listen and repeat.

4. What places in Exercise 2 are usually:
   a in a village?
   b in a town?

5. ▶ 72 Listen to four questions. Write the places.
   1 Is there a __ys__ near here?
   2 Is there a __ys__ near here?
   3 Is there a __no__ near here?
   4 Is there a __NO__ near here?

6. ▶ 73 Listen and match the answers (a–d) with questions (1–4) from Exercise 5.
   a Sorry. I don't know. I don't live here. _____
   b Yes. There's one next to the train station. _____
   c Yes. There's a Santander bank on this road. Down there. On the right. _____
   d Yes. There's one on this road. Down there. On the left. _____

34

GRAMMAR

> **Is there ... ? There's ...**
>
> A: **Is there** a supermarket near here?
> B: **There's** one next to the train station.
>
> A: **Is there** a bank near here?
> B: **There's** a Santander bank on this road.
>
> A: **Is there** a bank near here?
> B: No, **there isn't** (one).

7 Work in pairs. Try to remember the conversations in Exercise 6. Ask and answer the questions.

8 Work in pairs. Find five different things in the two pictures. Ask questions.

Student A: look at File 3 on page 81.

Student B: look at File 4 on page 82.

A: *Is there a bank?*
B: *Yes. Is there a cash machine?*
A: *No.*

> **G** For more about prepositions, see page 66 and do exercises 1 and 2 on page 67.

WRITING

9 Write five sentences about the different things.

*There's a hotel in Picture A, **but** there isn't one in Picture B.*

*There's a man in Picture A, **but** there's a woman in Picture B.*

LISTENING

10 ▶ 74 Listen. Where do they want to go?
 1 The woman needs a _cash machi_.
 2 The man wants to go to a _____ called Gema.
 3 The woman wants a _Car Park_.

11 ▶ 74 Listen again. Choose the correct word(s).
 1 The cash machine is:
   a 100 / 200 metres down the road.
   b in / next to the supermarket.
   c on the left / right.
 2 The pizza restaurant called Gema is:
   a on this / the next road.
   b the first / second restaurant.
   c on the left / right.
 3 The car park is on London Road.
   a London Road is the first / second road.
   b She needs to go left / right.
   c The car park is on the left / right.

12 ▶ 74 Listen again and read the conversations on page 88 to check your answers.

13 Work in pairs. Practise the conversations from Exercise 12.

DEVELOPING CONVERSATIONS

> **called**
> We use *called* to say the names of things and places.
> Do you know a restaurant **called** Gema?
> On Long Street, there's a bookshop **called** Bradley's.
> There's a nice clothes shop **called** Looking Good.

14 Complete the phrases with the names of places you know.

a restaurant called _____
a clothes shop called _____
a bookshop called _____
a hotel called _____
a village called _____
a town called _____
a _____ called _____

15 Work in pairs. Use your ideas from Exercise 14. Have conversations like this.

A: *Do you know a restaurant called Gema?*
B: *Yes, I like it.*

A: *Do you know a restaurant called Gema?*
B: *No. Where is it?*
A: *It's on Peter's Road.*
B: *Is it far? / Is it nice? / Is it expensive?*

CONVERSATION PRACTICE

16 Think about the town or city you are in now. Write:
 • three questions with *Is there ... near here?*
 • one question with *Do you know ...?*

17 Work in groups. Ask and answer the questions.

 75 For more practice, listen to another two examples.

Unit 4 Where and when?

WHEN ARE YOU FREE?

REVIEW AND SPEAKING

1 Choose two.
   - Look at the photos on pages 32 and 33. Test each other.
   - Ask about: a cash machine, a supermarket, a swimming pool, a restaurant.
   - Find out where people in the class work. What places from Exercise 2 on page 34 do they work in?

   A: *What do you do?*   A: *What do you do?*
   B: *I'm a teacher.*   B: *I work in a hospital.*
   A: *Where do you work?*   A: *Where is it?*
   B: *A school in Al Aln.* B: *In Festival Street.*

VOCABULARY Days and times of day

2 ▶ 76 Listen and repeat the days of the week.

   Monday   Wednesday   Friday   Sunday
   Tuesday   Thursday   Saturday

3 Complete 1–10 with a day or a time.
   1 Today: _____
   2 Tomorrow: _____
   3 Yesterday: _____
   4 Morning is from _____ to _____.
   5 Afternoon is from _____ to _____.
   6 Evening is from _____ to _____.
   7 Night is from _____ to _____.
   8 I have my English class on _____. It's from _____ to _____.
   9 The bank is always closed on _____.
   10 Supermarkets normally open at _____ in the morning.

4 Work in pairs. Discuss your ideas.

5 Write three days and times you are free.
   Monday morning
   Wednesday evening
   Saturday afternoon

6 Ask people in the class when they are free. Find two people who are free at the same time as you.
   A: *Are you free on Monday morning?*
   B: *No, sorry. I'm busy. Are you free on Saturday afternoon?*
   A: *Yes.*
   B: *Great. Me too.*

GRAMMAR

Adverbs of frequency

	Mon	Tue	Wed	Thur	Fri	Sat	Sun
I **always** go swimming in the morning.	x	x	x	x	x	x	x
I **normally** go swimming in the morning.	x	x		x		x	x
I **usually** go swimming in the morning.	x	x		x		x	x
I **sometimes** go swimming in the morning.			x			x	
I **never** go swimming in the morning.							

7 Work in pairs. Ask and answer the questions.
- What days do you work / go to class?
- What days are you normally free?
- What time do you start work/classes?
- What time do you normally go to bed?
- What time do you usually get up?

G For more practice, see Exercises 1 and 2 on page 67.

READING

8 Read about weekends in different countries. Which place is the same as your country?

9 Look at the words in red. Guess what they mean. Check in a dictionary.

▶ 77

THE END OF THE WORKING WEEK

Different countries have different weekends. The days depend on the religion and traditions of the country.

In Saudi Arabia, the weekend is usually Friday and Saturday, but some companies only have Friday for their weekend. In Indonesia, people normally only have a free day on Sunday.

In Colombia, people usually work 48 hours a week and lots of people only have Sunday free.

In Italy, people work 40 hours a week. A lot of people have Saturday and Sunday free, but children usually go to school on Saturday morning.

In Russia, Sunday is always a free day. Government offices are always open on Saturday and closed on Sunday and Monday. Other people are usually free on Saturday and Sunday.

People relax in Colombia.

10 Read again. Which sentences are true?
1 Weekends are always two days.
2 Saudi Arabia and Indonesia have the same weekend.
3 People in Colombia work a lot of hours and have a short weekend.
4 Children in Italy normally go to school from Monday to Saturday.
5 In Russia, offices are never open on Saturdays.

SPEAKING

11 Work in groups. Discuss the questions.
- What's the normal working week and weekend in your country?
- How many hours do people usually work? 40? More? Less?
- What is *your* working week – what days and how many hours?
- How many free days do *you* have a year?

12 Say how often you do these things at the weekend. When do you do them?
- go shopping for clothes / go shopping for food
- go to the beach / go to the pool
- go to a supermarket / go to a market
- go to church / go to mosque
- go to a village / go to another town or city
- get up early / get up late
- watch a film / watch football
- study English / study for university

I sometimes go shopping for clothes on Saturday afternoon.

I always go to the beach on Friday morning.

I never go to the market at the weekend.

People go to mosque in Indonesia.

Government offices in Russia

Unit 4 Where and when? 37

CAN YOU HELP ME?

SPEAKING

1 ▶78 Listen to the questions.

CLASS QUIZ

1. What time does the class start?
2. How long is the class?
3. What's the name or number of your classroom?
4. What floor is your classroom on?
5. Do you have a break? How long is it?
6. What's the name of your book?
7. Do you know the names of all the students in the class?
8. What's the first name of the teacher? And the family name of the teacher?
9. Who is the youngest person in the class?
10. Do you need to do homework? One hour a week? More? Less?
11. Is there anywhere to get a coffee in the school?
12. Can you have food or drink in the class?

2 Work in groups. Discuss the questions. Can you answer all the questions?

GRAMMAR

Can ...?
A: **Can** we have food or drink in the class?
B: *Sorry, you can't.*
A: **Can** I use your pen?
B: *Sure.*
A: **Can** you do Exercise 3 on page 121 for homework?
B: *OK.*

G For practice, see Exercises 1–3 on pages 67 and 68.

3 Look at some questions people ask in an English class. Who asks questions 1–7? Write *T* (teacher) or *S* (student).
 1 Can we have a break? S
 2 Can we have five more minutes?
 3 Can we have drinks in the class?
 4 Can you close the window?
 5 Can you do exercises six and seven?
 6 Can you help me?
 7 Can you wait a minute?

4 ▶79 Listen and repeat the questions from Exercise 3.

5 Work in pairs. Take turns.

 Student A: ask the questions from Exercise 3.

 Student B: give an answer.

 A: *Can we have a break?*
 B: *Sure/OK.*

6 Read these parts of five conversations. Complete them with the questions from Exercise 3.
 1 Student: It's difficult. _____?
   Teacher: Sure.
 2 Student: _____? I'm cold.
   Teacher: Is everybody else cold?
 3 Student A: Do you want to go and have a coffee?
   Student B: Sure. _____? I need to go to the toilet.
 4 Student: I can't come to class on Thursday.
   Teacher: OK. _____?
 5a Student: We're tired. _____?
 5b Student: _____?
   Teacher: Sorry. You can't.
   Student: OK. _____? We don't have time to drink our coffee.

7 ▶80 Listen to the full conversations and check.

VOCABULARY Classroom verbs

8 Match the phrases (1–8) with the pictures (a–h).

1 turn on the light
2 sit at the front
3 come in
4 use your tablet
5 play it again
6 leave early
7 write it on the board
8 share your book

9 Look at the situations (1–6). Write questions with *Can you* or *Can I* and phrases from Exercise 8.

1 I can't see the board. _____
2 I don't have my book. _____
3 Sorry, I'm late. _____
4 I don't feel well. _____
5 I don't know this word. _____
6 I don't understand. _____

10 Write more questions with *Can you* or *Can I* that:
- you ask the teacher
- the teacher asks you
- you ask another student

11 Work in pairs. Ask and answer your questions.

PRONUNCIATION AND REVIEW

12 ▶ 81 Listen to the sentences. They are fast. Write the number.

Is there a hospital near here?	_____
It's down this road on the right.	_____
It's at the end of this road on the left.	_____
There's one on the third floor.	_____
Do you know a town called Atrani?	_1_
I normally work late on Mondays.	_____
Are you free tomorrow night?	_____
There's one near here. The first road on the right.	_____

13 ▶ 82 Listen and check the answers. They are slow then fast.

14 Work in pairs. Practise the sentences.

15 Work in pairs. In one minute, say:
- days of the week and times of day.
- places in towns and cities.

G For more pronunciation, see Exercise 1 on page 68.

Unit 4 Where and when? **39**

VIDEO 2

MORNING

1 **Work in pairs. Answer the questions.**
   - Do you like mornings?
   - Do you usually feel tired? Happy? Hungry? Good or bad?

2 **Watch the first part of the video (0:00–0:56). Tick (✓) the countries you hear.**

Japan		Argentina	
America		Italy	
Turkey		Brazil	
Vietnam		Poland	
China		South Africa	

3 **Read the sentences from Part 2 of the video. Which country or person do you think each sentence is about?**

  1 He has an important job in a bank.
  A: *The man from Argentina?*
  B: *No, the man from Turkey. Nice clothes.*
  A: *Oh, yes.*
  2 Paolo is her first child. _____
  3 Children usually go to school on their own. _____
  4 The building is a new block of flats. _____
  5 He goes to the park every morning. _____
  6 She sells flowers in the street. _____
  7 The school gives the students breakfast for free. _____

4 **Watch the full video and check.**

5 **Work in pairs. Complete the sentences with the numbers.**

| 1st | 7.30 | 8 | 50 | $490 |
| 5 | 200 | 10 | 73 | 13 million |

  a This is Maiko. She's _____. She gets up at 6. It takes _____ minutes to get to school.
  b Paolo is her _____ child. He often wakes up at _____.
  c In America, _____ children don't have breakfast.
  d This is Serhat. He starts work at _____.
  e This is Yang. He's _____. He goes to the park every morning.
  f She has _____ flowers on her bike – or more!
  g This is Diego. He starts work at _____. He gets _____ a month.

6 **Watch the video again and check.**

SPEAKING

7 **Work in groups. Ask and answer the questions. Use a dictionary if you need to.**
   - What time do you get up?
   - What do you have for breakfast?
   - Do children sometimes have breakfast at school in your country?
   - Do you do exercise in the morning?
   - What time do you start work/school/university?
   - What things do people sell in the street in your town?

REVIEW 2

GRAMMAR

1 Choose the correct word(s).
1 Do you have *any / a* money?
2 *I don't / I'm not* well. I want to go home.
3 Can *you / we* help me? This is difficult.
4 I *sometimes / never* go to the cinema. I don't like it.
5 *Do you have / Have you* a pen?
6 *Is there / There is* a hospital in your town?
7 This bus *don't / not / doesn't* go to my area.
8 How long *it takes / does it take / it does take*?

2 Rewrite the sentences as negatives (–) or questions (?).
1 You have a mobile. (?)
2 There's a supermarket near here. (?)
3 They're French. (–)
4 It takes a long time. (–)
5 You need to do it today. (?)
6 She likes coffee. (–)

3 Complete the questions with *Can I* or *Can you*.
1 _____ use your pen?
2 _____ help me?
3 _____ do exercises 4 and 5 for homework?
4 I can't see the board. _____ sit at the front?
5 _____ wait a minute? I'm busy.
6 _____ help you?

4 Put the adverbs in the best place in the sentences.
1 Is the restaurant busy on Saturday night? (usually)
2 What time do you get up? (normally)
3 I go to the beach. I can't swim. (never)
4 I get up late on Sundays. (always)
5 I don't go out in the week. (normally)
6 I get the bus to work, but I get a taxi. (usually, sometimes)

5 ▶83 Listen and complete the sentences with one word in each space. Contractions (*I'm, don't*, etc.) are one word.
1 _____ she _____ _____ brothers or sisters?
2 I _____ _____ shopping _____ _____ _____ near here.
3 _____ _____ in my class at school.
4 Do you need _____ _____?
5 _____ _____ car park on the left.

6 ▶83 Work in pairs. Compare your answers. Listen again to check.

VOCABULARY

7 Match the verbs in the box with the correct groups of words (1–8).

get	share	take	use
go	sit	turn off	want

1 _____ your phone / the light
2 _____ a shower / a photo
3 _____ more free time / a new car
4 _____ next to the pool / at the front
5 _____ books / my food with you
6 _____ married / a coffee
7 _____ shopping / on holiday
8 _____ a dictionary / your tablets

8 Put the words into three groups: places, things or days / times of the day.

afternoon	charger	hotel	tomorrow
bag	church	map	toothpaste
bank	cinema	market	yesterday
brush	evening	Saturday	

9 Replace the words in italics with their opposites from the box.

busy	early	hot	morning
closed	good	left	new

1 The supermarket's *open*.
The supermarket's closed.
2 I'm *free* on Monday.
3 It's very *cold*.
4 I get up *late* on Sundays.
5 I go there every *evening*.
6 It's a *bad* film.
7 It's on the *right*.
8 They're my *old* shoes.

10 Complete the sentences with these adjectives.

difficult	hungry	married	tired
great	long	small	well

1 I'm _____ and I have two children.
2 Are you _____? Do you want a sandwich?
3 I like my flat, but it's very _____.
4 My homework is very _____. I can't do it.
5 Can I leave early? I'm not very _____.
6 I take the train to work. It usually takes a _____ time.
7 I'm _____. I need to have a break.
8 It's a _____ film. I love it.

Review 2 41

5 GOING PLACES

IN THIS UNIT YOU LEARN HOW TO:

- talk about good places to go
- say how to get to places
- talk about journeys
- buy train tickets
- ask about and say your plans
- say where and when to meet

WORDS FOR UNIT 5

1 **Look at the words and photos.**

1	go **out** in the **eve**ning	7	the **main square**
2	**v**isit a mus**eu**m	8	**wait** on the **plat**form
3	**use** the **ti**cket ma**chine**	9	a **bus stop**
4	**pay** by **card**	10	What **time's** the **flight**?
5	the **Old** Town	11	**sleep well**
6	**stay** at **home**	12	**play football**

2 ▶ 84 **Listen and repeat the words.**

3 **Work in pairs. Don't look at the words.**

Student A: say the number.

Student B: say the words.

Unit 5 Going places 43

GOOD PLACES TO GO

Visitors look at packets of food in the noodle museum in Yokohama, Japan.

SPEAKING

1 Work in pairs. Where do you go to:
- buy new clothes? *a clothes shop, a market*
- go out in the evening? *an area called Vestebro*
- get some money?
- have something to eat?
- have a walk?
- go swimming?
- sit and have a coffee?
- see some interesting art?
- see a film?

2 Choose four activities from Exercise 1. Say where you usually do these things.

I normally sit and have a coffee in a café called Music and Beans. It's near my house.

I usually get some money from a cash machine near my office.

LISTENING

3 ▶85 Listen to five conversations. Match conversations 1–5 with places a–e.

Conversation 1   a   a pool or a beach
Conversation 2   b   a good museum
Conversation 3   c   a cinema or the main square
Conversation 4   d   an area called Cihangir
Conversation 5   e   a street called Szeroka

4 ▶85 Listen again. Why do they want to go to each place? Choose an activity from Exercise 1.

5 ▶85 Listen again. Write the short words.
1 Are there any good shops _____ here?
2 There's a pool _____ this road. Or there's a beach _____ thirty minutes from here.
3 Not _____ the village. People go _____ the town. There are some nice places _____ the main square.
4 Try Ariel. It's _____ a street called Szeroka. _____ Kazimierz.
5 There's a good museum _____ the centre. It's _____ the station.

DEVELOPING CONVERSATIONS

best

We often use *best* to talk about one thing that is very good.

*What's the **best** restaurant?*

*Where's the **best** place to go?*

*It's **best** to take a bus.*

6 Work in groups. Think about your town/city. What's the best:

1 restaurant?   3 area?   5 hotel?
2 museum?   4 park?   6 market?

GRAMMAR

Are there … ? / There are …

A: **Are there** any good shops near here?
B: Yes. **There are** lots of nice places in Cihangir.

A: **Are there** any places to go out in the evening here?
B: Yes. **There are** some good places on South Street.

7 Choose the correct word(s).

1. A: I want to have a coffee. *Is there / Are there* a nice café near here?
   B: Yes. *There's / There are* four or five different places in Nova Street.
2. A: I want to have something to eat. *Is there / Are there* any good restaurants near here?
   B: Yes. Try Via Garibaldi. *There's / There are* some nice places there.
3. A: I need to get some money. Is there *a / any* bank near here?
   B: Yes, *there's / there are* one down this road.
4. A: I want to visit some places. Are there *a / any* interesting places near here?
   B: Well, *there's / there are* a museum in the Old Town. Lots of people go there.

8 ▶86 Listen to the sentences. They are fast then slow.

1. Are there any good shops near here?
2. Are there any nice places to eat?
3. Are there any markets in town?
4. There are some nice cafés in the main square.
5. There are lots of good places to go.
6. There are normally a lot of people there.

ⓖ For more practice, see Exercises 1–3 on pages 68 and 69.

9 Work in pairs. Practise the sentences.

VOCABULARY Getting there

10 Match the phrases (1–8) with the pictures (a–h).

1. get off
2. get a taxi
3. go home
4. take the metro
5. walk to work
6. change trains
7. wait for the bus
8. take the red line

WRITING

11 Write true sentences about you and where you live. Use the ideas here. Change the words in red.

The metro in my town is very cheap.
I usually take the train to work.
I usually wait about ten minutes for the train.
To get to my house, take the metro. It's the blue line. Get off at Rocafort.
I never walk to the shops.
I sometimes get a taxi to go home.

CONVERSATION PRACTICE

12 ▶87 Listen to the complete conversations from Exercise 3. Answer the questions.

	How do you get there?	How long does it take?
1	walk	
2		30 minutes
3		
4		
5		

13 Work in pairs. You are in your partner's home. Write three questions to ask about places.

I want to buy some clothes. Are there any good shops near here?

14 Student A: give your questions to your partner.
Student B: think of answers and directions.

15 Have conversations. Take turns.

Student A	Student B
I want to …. Is/Are there …?	
	There's / There are …. [Say where.]
How do you get there?	
	It's best to take … / It takes …
OK. Thanks.	Or you can …. It takes …

▶88 For more practice, listen to another example.

Unit 5 Going places 45

HAVE A GOOD TRIP!

REVIEW AND SPEAKING

1 Write two nouns next to each verb. Work in groups. Compare.
   1 take _____
   2 get off _____
   3 visit _____
   4 wait for _____
   5 buy _____

2 Ask other students the questions. Add one more question.
   How do you normally get here / to school / to work?
   How long does it take?

READING

3 Read the first line of the text. Do you think trains are best? Why? / Why not?

4 Read about train travel. Match paragraphs 1–3 with photos a–c.

5 Match sentences a–c with paragraphs 1–3.
   a A train journey can be a holiday.
   b There are some beautiful stations.
   c You can get great views from a train.

▶ 89

WHY I LOVE TRAIN TRAVEL

Planes are fast, buses are cheap, but trains are the best. Here are three reasons:

1 This is Grand Central in New York. It is more than 100 years old. It has 44 platforms and 750,000 people use the station every day.

2 You can sit and see the world outside. Sometimes you can see beautiful mountains or the sea. This is the train from Fort William to Mallaig in Scotland. This line is in the Harry Potter films. It takes 80 minutes and a single ticket only costs £7.50 ($10).

3 Some train journeys take a long time and you sleep on the train. You can travel for four days in Kyushu, Japan on the private Seven Star train. There are only 28 passengers. They can sit and talk and have dinner together. You can get off and visit some interesting places. It costs $14,000 for four nights. Or you can have a cheap holiday on the train from Moscow to Vladivostok in the east of Russia. It takes six days and seventeen hours. That's a lot of time to make friends and it only costs $160 in third class!

46

6 Read again. Answer the questions.
1 Where is Grand Central?
2 Where is Fort William?
3 Where is the Seven Star Train?
4 Which journey is very expensive?
5 Which journey is very long?

7 Look at the words in red. Guess what they mean. Check in a dictionary.

8 Work in pairs. Do you want to visit Grand Central or go on each train journey? Why? / Why not?

VOCABULARY Buying tickets

9 ▶ 90 Listen and repeat the words and phrases. Tick (✓) the words you know.

cash	a ma**chine**	re**turn**
change trains	the **next train**	se**cond class**
en**ter** your **num**ber	**pay** by **card**	**sin**gle
first class	a re**ceipt**	a **tic**ket

10 Complete the conversation between an assistant (A) and a tourist (T). Use one word from the box in each space.

A: Do you want to buy a ¹_____?

T: Er ... yes.

A: You can use the ²_____ over here. You can pay by cash or ³_____ and you don't need to wait.

T: Oh, OK. Is the machine in German?

A: Yes, but I can help you. Come with me.

T: OK.

A: Where are you going?

T: Lausanne.

A: ⁴_____ or return?

T: Return.

A: For now, right?

T: Yes. And back on Monday.

A: Yes, fine. ⁵_____ class? Second class?

T: Second class is fine.

A: OK. Do you want a receipt?

T: Yes, please.

A: Put your card in here and enter your ⁶_____.

T: OK.

A: And here are your tickets and ⁷_____.

T: When's the ⁸_____ train?

A: 9.47. From platform 8.

T: Sorry. Which platform?

A: 8 – at 9.47.

T: OK. Thank you for your help.

A: You're welcome. Have a good day.

11 ▶ 91 Listen and check.

12 Work in pairs. Practise the conversation in Exercise 10.

DEVELOPING CONVERSATIONS

Where are you going?

A: **Where are you going?**

T: *Lausanne.*

A: *Single or return?*

A: *Is this the stop for the 98 bus?*

B: *Yes.* **Where are you going?**

A: *The museum.*

13 Think of the town or city you are in now. Write down five places you want to go to.

14 Work in pairs. Take turns. Have conversations like this.

A: *Where are you going?*

B: *The City museum.*

A: *You need to take the 73 bus. / You can walk there.*

SPEAKING

15 Work in pairs. Practise the conversation in Exercise 10 two more times. Take turns to start.

First time: Change the information in red.

Second time: Change the information in blue.

Unit 5   Going places   47

GOOD PLAN!

LISTENING

1. What do you normally do:
   - after your class?
   - after work?
   - on holiday?

2. ▶ 92 Listen to three conversations about plans. Write the number of the conversations (1, 2 and 3) next to who is talking (a or b).

   a friends at a hotel in the evening _____
   b friends at the end of a class _____

3. ▶ 93 Listen to the sentences. Repeat them.

   a I need some money. _____
   b I need to study. _____
   c I need to eat something. _____
   d I'm going home. _____
   e I'm going to bed. _____
   f I'm going to have a coffee. ___1___
   g I'm going to meet a friend. _____
   h I'm going to stay here. _____

4. ▶ 92 Listen to the conversations from Exercise 2 again. Write the number of the conversation next to each sentence (a–h) in Exercise 3.

5. In which conversations are the two people going to do:
   a the same thing?   b different things?

GRAMMAR

Talking about plans: I'm/We're going …

Plan	Where / What	When
I'm going We're going	home to the gym to the cinema	now. this afternoon. at six.
I'm going We're going	to have a coffee to meet a friend to see a film to play football	tonight. tomorrow. on Saturday. after the class.

6. Put the words in the correct order.
   1. tonight / I'm going / to meet my brother
   2. we're going / this afternoon / to the park
   3. to the beach / we're going / on Sunday
   4. now / to have a coffee / I'm going
   5. tomorrow night / we're going / to have a party
   6. I'm going / tomorrow morning / to the pool / with some friends

7. ▶ 94 Listen and check.

8 Work in pairs. Use the ideas from Exercise 6. Invite your partner.

A: *I'm going to meet my brother tonight. Do you want to come?*

B: *Sorry, I can't.* or B: *OK. Great!*

9 Write more plans. Use a dictionary if you need to.

_____ after the class.
_____ tonight.
_____ tomorrow.
_____ on Saturday.
_____ next week.

10 Work in groups. Say your plans.

11 Tell the class who is going to do the same thing.

We're all going for a coffee after the class!

Aslim and I are going to the park on Saturday.

G For more practice, see Exercises 1–4 on page 69.

GRAMMAR

Asking about plans: *going* and *doing*

	Are you **going**?
What time Where	**are** you **going**?
What	**are** you **doing** after the class? **are** you **doing** tonight?

12 Write the questions.

1 A: I'm going to the beach on Saturday. Do you want to come?
 B: _____?
 A: Five or six in the afternoon.

2 A: I'm going to have a walk later.
 B: _____?
 A: Around the Old Town.

3 A: _____ tonight?
 B: I'm going to see a film. Do you want to come?
 A: Sorry. I can't. I need to study.

4 A: _____ to Dieter's party tomorrow?
 B: Yes. _____?
 A: Yes. Do you want to share a taxi?

13 ▶ 95 Listen and repeat the questions in the Grammar box.

G For more practice, see Exercises 1 and 2 on pages 69 and 70.

14 Work in pairs. Ask about plans from Exercise 9. Ask questions to know more.

DEVELOPING CONVERSATIONS

I'll meet you

We use *I'll meet you* to say where and when to meet.

I'll meet you here in ten minutes.
I'll meet you outside.
I'll meet you here at 6.
I'll meet you at the airport

15 ▶ 96 Listen. Choose the correct word(s).

1 I'll meet you at *the restaurant / the hotel*.
2 I'll meet you at *the airport / the station*.
3 I'll meet you *at the bus stop / outside* at six.
4 I'll meet you *here / there* in ten minutes.
5 I'll meet you here at *three / five* o'clock.

16 Say the sentences from Exercise 15 and answer.

A: *I'll meet you at the bus stop at six.*

B: *OK* or B: *Can we meet at six thirty?*

17 Ask other students about their plans. Invite someone to do something.

Student A	Student B
What are you doing [when]?	
	I'm going ... Do you want to come?
[Question]	
	[Answer]
OK.	
	Great. I'll meet you ...
Great.	

PRONUNCIATION AND REVIEW

18 ▶ 97 Listen to the sentences. They are fast. Write the number.

How do you get there? _____
What time are you going? _____
When's the next train? _____
Where are you going? _____
We need to get off at the next stop. _____
We need to change at Red Square. _____
I'll meet you at six. _____
I'm going to meet a friend. __1__

19 ▶ 98 Listen and check the answers. They are slow then fast.

20 Practise the sentences.

21 Work in pairs. In one minute, say:
- words for buying tickets and travelling by train
- things you are going to do next weekend

G For more pronunciation, see Exercise 1 on page 70.

Unit 5 Going places 49

6 AWAY FROM HOME

IN THIS UNIT YOU LEARN HOW TO:

- say there's a problem
- say *don't worry* and *that's OK*
- ask how something was
- check in to a hotel
- talk about your stay
- ask what people did

WORDS FOR UNIT 6

1 Look at the words and photos.

1	on the **top floor**	8	a lot of **tra**ffic
2	**keys**	9	make a **boo**king
3	**clean** the **bath**room	10	make **di**nner
4	**play mu**sic	11	**stay** in a **hos**tel
5	**right** and **wrong**	12	what's the **WiFi pass**word?
6	do **ex**ercise	13	a **bu**sy **street**
7	**take** the **lift**	14	**mo**dern **art**

2 ▶ 99 Listen and repeat the words.

3 Work in pairs. Don't look at the words.

Student A: say the number.

Student B: say the words.

Unit 6 Away from home 51

a Rain on holiday

b People wait for their late flight.

HOW WAS YOUR FLIGHT?

VOCABULARY Problems

1 Look at the photos (a–d). Say if each is a big problem or a small problem.

2 ▶ 100 Listen and repeat the words. Tick (✓) the words you know.

| late | no-one | problem | tired |
| noise | nowhere | rain | wrong |

V For more about pronouns like *no-one* and *nowhere*, see page 76.

3 Complete 1–8 with the words from Exercise 2.
  1 I have a _____ at work. I need to work late.
  2 I can't sleep. There's a lot of _____ outside my room.
  3 The weather's very bad. There's a lot of _____.
  4 The flight is two hours _____. We need to wait in the airport.
  5 We need help, but there's _____ here.
  6 There are a lot of people here. There's _____ to sit.
  7 I'm going to bed early. I'm very _____.
  8 We're going the _____ way. This isn't the right train!

4 ▶ 101 Listen and check.

5 Look at Exercise 3 again. Choose one problem you often have, one problem you sometimes have and one problem you never have.
  I need to work late: I often have this problem.

LISTENING

6 ▶ 102 Dana meets Bryan at the airport. Choose the correct word(s), then listen and check.
  A: Bryan. Great to see you!
  B: Hi, Dana. ¹*How / Who* are you?
  A: Great.
  B: Sorry ²*we're / I'm* late. There was a problem in London.
  A: Don't worry. It was on the airport website.
  B: Oh, good.
  A: How was the flight?
  B: ³*Very / Not very* good. The weather was bad.
  A: Oh, I'm sorry. Are you tired?
  B: Yeah. Where are ⁴*you / we* going now?
  A: To the hotel and then we can have something to eat.
  B: Oh, sorry. I had dinner on the plane. ⁵*I'm / I'm not* hungry.
  A: That's OK. ⁶*Do / Are* you want to stay in the hotel?
  B: Is that OK? I did a lot yesterday and I went to bed late.
  A: Of course! We ⁷*can / are* go out tomorrow.
  B: Great. Thanks.

GRAMMAR

Past simple: common irregular verbs

Present	Past	
is	was	There **was** a problem in London.
are	were	We **were** late.
have/has	had	I **had** dinner on the plane.
go/goes	went	I **went** to bed late.
do/does	did	I **did** a lot yesterday.

7 ▶ 103 Listen and repeat the past forms in the box.

8 Work in pairs. Look at the verb list on page 74. Practise the conversation from Exercise 6.

9 Complete the sentences with *did, had, was, were,* or *went*.
  1 A: How was your day?
     B: Bad. I _____ a lot of problems at work.
  2 A: How was your day?
     B: Good. I _____ a lot of work.
  3 A: How was your flight?
     B: Bad. It _____ four hours late!

52

c A lot of noise outside the hotel

d Tired after a busy day

4 A: How was your journey?
  B: Bad. We _____ the wrong way. There was a lot of traffic.

5 A: How was your holiday?
  B: Great. We _____ very good weather. We _____ to the beach every day.

6 A: How was your hotel?
  B: Great. The rooms _____ very nice.

7 A: I _____ shopping yesterday.
  B: How was it?
  A: OK. It was busy.

8 A: I _____ a party last weekend. I was 25.
  B: How was it?
  A: Great. All my friends were there.

10 Complete each sentence in two ways.
   I went to _____ yesterday / last night.
   I had _____ yesterday / last night.

11 Tell your partner your sentences. Your partner asks *How was it?*
   A: *I went to the cinema yesterday.*
   B: *How was it?*
   A: *Good.*

G For more practice, see Exercises 1 and 2 on page 70.

DEVELOPING CONVERSATIONS

Don't worry / That's OK
A: *Sorry, I'm late! There was a problem in London.*
B: ***Don't worry!** I know.*
A: *Sorry. I'm not hungry.*
B: ***That's OK.***

12 Put the words in brackets in the correct order to make a second sentence.
   1 Sorry I'm late. (had / at work / I / a problem)
   2 Sorry I'm late. (the wrong place / went to / I)
   3 Sorry I'm late. (on the bus / was / there / a problem)

13 Take turns to say the sentences from Exercise 12. Reply with *don't worry* or *that's OK*.

14 ▶ 104 Listen and complete the sentences.
   1 Sorry I _____ come to class on Monday.
   2 Sorry. I _____ have any money.
   3 Sorry. I _____ very early!
   4 Sorry the room _____ very big.
   5 Sorry. I _____ know the answer.

15 Complete your own sentences.
   Sorry I'm late. _____.
   Sorry I'm late. I had a problem at home.
   Sorry. _____.
   Sorry. I don't have my book.

16 Work in pairs. Say your sentences from Exercise 15 to different students. Reply.

CONVERSATION PRACTICE

17 Write an answer to the questions. Use a dictionary if you need to.
   • How was your journey/flight?
   • How was your day?
   • How was your holiday?

18 Work in pairs. Have conversations like this.

Student A	Student B
Hi. How are you?	
	[Answer] And you?
[Answer]. Sorry I'm late.	
	[Answer].
How was _____?	
	[Answer] How was _____?
[Answer]	

▶ 105 For more practice, listen to another example.

Unit 6 Away from home 53

WE LOVED IT

REVIEW AND SPEAKING

1 Test each other on the words on page 51.

2 Ask and answer six *How* questions.

How are you?   How was the last class?
How's work?   How was your weekend?
How do you get here?   How was your day yesterday?

VOCABULARY Hotels and checking in

3 Complete the sentences with these words.

ad**dress**	**break**fast	**lift**	**pass**word
bags	check **out**	**num**ber	**rooms**
booking	**key**	**pass**port	

1 Good evening. Do you have any _____ for tonight?
2 Hi. We have a _____. My name's Kim Jae-Sung.
3 Can I have your _____, please?
4 Can you write your name and _____ here? And sign here?
5 Do you need help with your _____?
6 Here's your key. Your room _____ is 351.
7 What time do we need to _____?
8 I'm sorry there's no _____. The stairs are over there.
9 What time is _____ in the morning?
10 What's the _____ for the WiFi?

4 ▶ 106 Listen and check your answers.

5 ▶ 107 Listen to someone checking in. Tick (✓) the sentences in Exercise 3 you hear.

6 ▶ 107 Listen again. What's the problem (a, b or c)?
  a The restaurant is closed.
  b He needs to pay for breakfast.
  c They don't have his booking.

7 Work in pairs. Practise the conversation.
  A: Hi.
  B: Hello. How can I help you?
  A: We have a booking. My name's [Name].
  B: OK. Yes. Can I have your passport?
  A: Sure.
  B: Can you write your name and address here? And sign here?
  A: Here? OK.
  B: Here's your key. Your room number is [Number].

8 Work in a new pair. Practise the conversation again, then continue the conversation. Use one or two questions from Exercise 3.

READING AND GRAMMAR

9 Is each sentence (1–6) about a hotel or a hostel?
  1 There were eight beds in each room.
  2 We shared a bathroom.
  3 It had four stars. It was $190 a night.
  4 I talked to the other people in my room.
  5 There was a swimming pool on the top floor.
  6 We stayed in the best place in the city centre.

10 Look at the Grammar box on page 55. Notice how we form the regular past simple forms. Follow the rule to complete the other two sentences in the box.

Regular past simple endings

Present	Past	
stay(s)	stay**ed**	We **stayed** in the best place.
talk(s)	talk**ed**	He **talked** to us.
rain(s)	_____	It _____ a lot.
share(s)	shar**ed**	We **shared** a bathroom.
love(s)	_____	I _____ it.

G For more practice, see Exercises 1 and 2 on page 71.

11 Read about the three places in Costa Rica. Which do you like best?

12 Read again. Match sentences a–c with the three places in the text.
   a The weather wasn't very good one day.
   b There wasn't any noise.
   c There were lots of people and it wasn't expensive.

13 Look at the words in red. Guess what they mean. Check in a dictionary.

14 Work in groups. Answer the questions.
   • Do you want to go to Costa Rica? Why? / Why not?
   • What places do you want to go to: in your country? in a different country?

GRAMMAR

Past simple negatives

Positive	Negative
There **were** a lot of people.	There **weren't** a lot of people.
The weather **was** good.	The weather **wasn't** good.
It **had** a restaurant.	It **didn't have** a restaurant.
We **saw** a lot.	We **didn't see** a lot.

15 Make the sentences negative.
   1 It was a nice place.
   2 We had a car.
   3 We visited San José.
   4 There were a lot of hotels.
   5 There was a lot of noise.
   6 It rained.

G For more practice, see Exercises 1 and 2 on page 71.

WRITING

16 Write about a place you went to on holiday. Change the words in red. Add two more sentences with your own ideas.

   I went to Cairo. I stayed there for five days.
   I stayed in a hotel called the Safary.
   It's near the centre.
   It was cheap but nice.
   The weather wasn't good. It was very hot.

A forest and beach in Nosara

Arenal volcano and lake near Fortuna

▶ 108

A HOLIDAY IN COSTA RICA

Tell us about your stay in Costa Rica.

SELINA HOSTEL $9/night   4/5
I stayed in San José for six days. The hostel was good. It's near the city centre and the modern art museum. I shared a room with nine other people. The room was clean and the other people were nice to talk to. The café in the hostel was OK and sometimes there was a band.

TIERRA MAGNÍFICA $365/night   5/5
We went to Nosara last December. We stayed in this small five-star place. It's in a forest, but you can see the beach from the hotel. There weren't a lot of people. It was quiet. The service and the food were great. We loved it.

HOTEL REGINA $38/night   4/5
This great place is in the centre of Fortuna and we had a view of the Arenal Volcano from our room. We didn't have dinner in the hotel. There was a nice restaurant in the same street. One day, we did a tour of the volcano. It rained and we didn't see a lot. Another day we went swimming in a lake. It was beautiful.

Unit 6   Away from home

WHAT DID YOU DO?

People dance in the streets of Buenos Aires in Argentina.

SPEAKING

1 Work in pairs. Say:
   - the time of the day you like best: morning, afternoon, evening or night.
   - one thing you usually do at each time of day and one thing you never do.
   - the meal you like best: breakfast, lunch or dinner.
   - one thing you usually have and one thing you always have for each meal.

LISTENING

2 ▶ 109 Lucy and Dom are in a hostel. Listen to the first part of their conversation. Choose the correct word(s).
   1 It's the *morning* / *evening*.
   2 They talk about their *breakfast* / *dinner*.
   3 They talk about what Lucy did *during the day* / *last night*.

3 ▶ 110 Listen to the first and second parts of the conversation. Put Lucy (L) or Dom (D) next to sentences 1–8.
   1 I went to bed late. _____
   2 I went to bed early. _____
   3 I didn't eat a lot for breakfast. _____
   4 I didn't go out. _____
   5 I walked round the Old Town. _____
   6 I talked to some people after dinner. _____
   7 I danced a lot. _____
   8 I didn't feel well. _____

4 ▶ 111 Listen to the third part of the conversation. What are they doing today?
   a They are going shopping after breakfast.
   b They are going to the modern art museum together.
   c Dom is going to the modern art museum and Lucy is going to the beach.

5 Work in pairs. Discuss the questions. When you are on holiday:
   - do you talk to other people? Who? Where? When?
   - do you usually stay in a hostel or a hotel? In the city or near the beach?
   - do you like: walks in the Old Town? / dancing? / modern art? / other museums?

6 ▶ 112 Listen to the questions from the conversation. Complete each question with one word.
   1 _____ I sit here?
   2 How _____ your breakfast?
   3 What did you _____?
   4 How _____ you? Did you sleep well?
   5 What _____ you do?
   6 _____ did you go?
   7 _____ was it?
   8 _____ it busy?
   9 And you? What did you _____ last night?
   10 _____ you OK now?
   11 So, what _____ you doing today?
   12 _____ you want to go together?
   13 When are you _____?
   14 _____ time is it now?

56

10 Complete the conversations about yesterday. Make questions with *did you* or *do you*.

1 A: I went shopping.
   B: _____ (What / buy?)
2 A: I went to work.
   B: _____ (Where / work?)
3 A: I went out.
   B: _____ (Where / go?)
4 A: I went to my classes at the university.
   B: _____ (What / study?)
5 A: I went to the beach.
   B: _____ (stay there all day?)
6 A: I stayed at home.
   B: _____ (What / do?)
7 A: I watched TV.
   B: _____ (What / see?)
8 A: I went to the gym.
   B: _____ (go every day?)

11 ▶114 Listen and check your answers.

12 Work in pairs. Take turns to start conversations from Exercise 10. Add answers to the questions.

1 A: *I went shopping.*
   B: *What did you buy?*
   A: *Some clothes.*

13 Think of your answers to these questions.
   • What did you do yesterday? last weekend?
   • What did you do on your last holiday?

14 Ask and answer the questions from Exercise 13. Ask other questions to get more information.
   A: *What did you do yesterday?*
   B: *I went to work.*
   A: *What do you do?*

PRONUNCIATION AND REVIEW

15 ▶115 Listen to the sentences. They are fast. Write the missing word.
   1 How was your _____?
   2 I had a very busy _____.
   3 We stayed in a _____.
   4 We had a great view of the _____.
   5 What's the password for the _____?
   6 What did you do last _____?
   7 I met some _____.
   8 I went to the _____.

16 Work in pairs. Say the sentences from Exercise 15, but change the last word.

17 Try to remember the answers in Exercise 6.

18 Work in pairs. In one minute say:
   • past verbs • words about problems

G For more revision and pronunciation, see Exercises 1–4 on page 72.

GRAMMAR

Past simple questions

What	did you	do (last night / yesterday)? have (for breakfast/dinner)?
Where	did you	go?
What time		go to bed? get here?
	Did you	sleep well? go out (last night)?
How **was** it?		
Was it busy?		
Were you tired?		

7 ▶113 Learn to say these questions. Listen and repeat what you hear.
   What did you do last night?
   What did you do yesterday?

8 Ask different people in the class the two questions from Exercise 7.

9 Who in the class did one of these things?
   • went to work/classes   • did some exercise/sport
   • stayed at home   • met a friend / some friends
   • went out
   • went shopping   • watched TV

G For more practice, see Exercises 1–4 on pages 71 and 72.

Unit 6 Away from home 57

VIDEO 3

ANCIENT LAND

A very big library

A very old temple

A great museum

1 **Look at the photos. Discuss the questions.**
- Do you know a country where you can see all these things?
- Do you know the place well?
- What else can you see there?

2 **Watch the video. Complete the table with the words.**

| Alexandria | cafés | great art | mosques |
| beach | Cairo | Luxor | pyramids |

City	Famous sight	Other things to see
	the museum	
	the library	
	the temple	

3 **Watch the video again. Are these sentences true (T) or false (F)? Correct the false ones.**
1 Around twelve million people live in Cairo.
2 You can see Pharaoh Tutankhamun at the Egyptian Museum.
3 There are seventeen pyramids in Egypt.
4 The pyramids at Saqqara are five thousand years old.
5 It takes four hours by train to get to Alexandria from Cairo.
6 The library has books in Arabic, French and German.
7 Luxor is in the north of the country.
8 Before it was called Thebes and it was the capital of Egypt.

4 **Match the verbs (1–6) with the words and phrases (a–f) to make phrases from the video.**

1 see   a on the beach
2 rent   b big temples
3 take   c great art
4 relax   d the sun go down
5 build   e a boat
6 create   f three hours to get there

5 **Watch the video again to check your answers.**

SPEAKING

6 **Work in pairs. Discuss the questions.**
- Do you want to visit Egypt?
- What are the three best towns or cities to visit in your country?
- What can you see and do in each place?

58

REVIEW 3

GRAMMAR

1 Choose the correct word(s).

1 *Is / Are* there any good places to eat near here?
2 There *is / are* a nice Italian restaurant in the main square.
3 *Did / Were* you go out last night?
4 What *you are doing / are you doing* after class?
5 I went to Denmark. The weather *wasn't / weren't / didn't* good.
6 It wasn't busy. There *weren't / wasn't / didn't* a lot of people there.
7 *There are / There is / Have* lots of good shops in this area.
8 I'm going *play / for to play / to play* football this afternoon.

2 Complete the text with the past simple of the verbs.

Last year I ¹_____ (go) on holiday to Tunisia. It ²_____ (be) great. We ³_____ (stay) in a small village near the beach. Our rooms ⁴_____ (be) very nice and there ⁵_____ (not / be) a lot of noise. There ⁶_____ (not / be) a lot of people there. Every evening we ⁷_____ (have) dinner in a very nice restaurant and it ⁸_____ (not / rain) for a week. We ⁹_____ (talk) to lots of very nice people. I ¹⁰_____ (love) it. I want to go again.

3 Write questions to complete the conversations. Use the words in brackets.

1 A: _____? (where / you / go)
   B: Home. I'm tired. I need to sleep.
2 A: _____ after class? (what / you / do)
   B: I'm going to meet a friend. We're going to see a film.
3 A: Kenzo is going to have a party on Friday.
   B: I know. _____? (you / go)
   A: Yes, I am.
4 A: _____ last night? (what / you / do)
   B: We went out. It was fun. I didn't sleep a lot!
   A: _____? (where / you / go)
   B: We went to see a band. They were great.

4 ▶ 116 Listen and complete the sentences.

1 _____ _____ _____ to the museum yesterday?
2 I'm _____ _____ _____ some friends this afternoon.
3 _____ _____ _____ good places to eat in Kalamaki.
4 _____ _____ _____ you _____ to bed last night?
5 We _____ good weather on Saturday. We _____ _____ the beach.

5 ▶ 116 Work in pairs. Compare your answers. Listen again to check.

VOCABULARY

6 Match the verbs in the box with the correct groups of words (1–8).

get	have	play	stay
go	need	see	take

1 _____ a film / some interesting art
2 _____ the blue line / the lift
3 _____ at home / in a hostel
4 _____ a walk / a party
5 _____ to bed late / swimming
6 _____ a taxi / a great view
7 _____ football / some music
8 _____ to study tonight / some more money

7 Put the words into three groups: buying tickets, hotels or problems.

a lot of rain	nowhere to sit	return
a lot of traffic	passport	second class
check out	password	single
key	platform	the wrong way

8 Complete the text with these words.

change	get off	long	take
costs	line	metro	wait

I usually ¹_____ the train to work. The ²_____ here is expensive, but it's good. I usually ³_____ three or four minutes for my train. I take the red ⁴_____ and then I ⁵_____ trains at Holborn. I ⁶_____ at Green Park. It doesn't take ⁷_____ – about thirty minutes most days – and it ⁸_____ about £150 a month.

9 Complete the sentences with these verbs.

clean	enter	sleep	walk
do	pay	visit	write

1 Is it far? Can we _____ there?
2 Is there a park near here? I want to _____ some exercise.
3 Here's the machine. Can you _____ your number, please?
4 Can you _____ your name and address here, please?
5 We're going to _____ the museum in the Old Town this afternoon.
6 I'm sorry. There's a problem with the bathroom. Can you _____ it, please?
7 Can I _____ by card?
8 Good morning. Did you _____ well?

Review 3 59

GRAMMAR REFERENCE

1 BE

'M, 'S, 'RE
Pronouns

I	you
he	she
it	we
they	they

Exercise 1
▶ 188 Listen and repeat.

be

am
I'm Andrew. (= I am)

are
You're Naomi, right? (= You are)
We're from Saudi Arabia. (= We are)
They're from China. (= They are)

is
She's a doctor. (= She is)   He's my boss. (= He is)
It's good. (= It is)   This is my brother.
That's right. (= That is)
My daughter's 6. (= My daughter is)

Exercise 2
▶ 188 Listen and write the missing word.
1 _____'m Juan. Nice to meet you.
2 _____ is my teacher, Lena.
3 _____'s my sister.
4 _____'re in the same class.
5 _____'s nice.
6 Who are _____?
7 What's _____?
8 _____ son is three today.

Exercise 3
Write the sentences with the *'m, 're, 's* forms.
1 I am from Berlin. *I'm from Berlin.*
2 He is from London. _____
3 My name is Cathy. _____
4 We are friends. _____
5 They are in my class. _____
6 You are in class 6. _____
7 She is my teacher _____
8 That is right. _____

	Stella. Javier.	name
	OK. good.	adjective
I'm	a teacher. her father.	person/job
	from London. in the class.	place

Exercise 4
Write four sentences about you and four sentences about another person. Use a dictionary if you need to.

I'm _____
I'm _____
I'm _____
I'm _____
My _____'s _____.
My _____'s _____.
My _____'s _____.
My _____'s _____.

QUESTIONS WITH *BE*

am
I'm sorry.   What class **am I** in?

are
You're right.   How **are you**?
We're in class 1.   Where **are we**?
They're very nice.   Where **are they** from?

is
He's nice.   How old **is he**?
She's a teacher.   Who **is she**?
It's ten o'clock.   How much **is it**?
This is my book.   Who **is this**?
Your son's nice.   How old **is your son**?

Exercise 1

Complete the sentences with *are*, *is* or *'s*.

1. A: Where _____ he from?
   B: Kuwait.
2. A: How old _____ you?
   B: Twenty.
3. A: What _____ your name?
   B: Maria.
4. A: How long _____ the class?
   B: Three hours.
5. A: How old _____ your brother?
   B: Seventeen.
   A: _____ he here?
   B: No, he's at school.
6. A: Where _____ your father from, Reo?
   B: Aizuwakamatsu.
   A: _____ it a big place?
   B: No. It _____ very small.

Exercise 2

Put the words in the correct order to make questions.

1. you / where / are / from   *Where are you from?*
2. much / how / are / they
3. he / is / who
4. how / are / old / you
5. their / what / names / are
6. you / how / are
7. what / is / time / bus / the

Exercise 3

Match the answers with the questions from Exercise 2.

a. Khalid and Fatima.
b. Dubai.
c. $25.50.
d. Twenty-one.
e. My husband.
f. Eleven o'clock.
g. Good, thanks.

Yes/No questions and short answers

Am I OK here?	Yes, you **are**.	No, you**'re not**.
Are you OK?	Yes, I **am**.	No, I**'m not**.
Are we in the right class?	Yes, you **are**.	No, you**'re not**.
Are they from Tokyo?	Yes, they **are**.	No, they**'re not**.
Is he 16?	Yes, he **is**.	No, he**'s not**.
Is your son at school?	Yes, he **is**.	No, he**'s not**.
Is she your teacher?	Yes, she **is**.	No, she**'s not**.
Is it expensive?	Yes, it **is**.	No, it**'s not**.
Is this your book?	Yes, it **is**.	No, it**'s not**.

Exercise 4

Write a short answer to these questions.

1. Are you Olivia? (✓)   *Yes, I am.*
2. Is your name Omar? (✗)   *No, it's not.*
3. Am I late? (✓)
4. Are we in this class? (✓)
5. Are you OK? (✗)
6. Is he sixteen? (✓)
7. Is she your wife? (✗)
8. Is it right? (✗)
9. Are they your mother and father? (✓)
10. Is this your bag? (✓)

HIS, HER, OUR, THEIR

Possessive adjectives and *'s*

my cat	**your** cat	**his** cat
her cat	**our** cat	**their** cat
Sheila**'s** cat	Henry**'s** cat	Peter and John**'s** cat

Exercise 1

A Complete the sentences with *my*, *your*, etc. or [name]*'s*.

1. *His* name is Karim.
2. *Karen's* husband is a teacher.
3. _____ name's Ulla.
4. _____ address is 15 New Road.
5. Where's _____ flat?
6. When's _____ party?
7. What's _____ name?
8. Is _____ new baby a boy or a girl?   Liam

Grammar reference   61

9 What's _____ name?
10 What's _____ phone number?

B ▶ 189 Listen and check.

Exercise 2
Choose the correct word(s).
1 *I* / *My* am from Oman.
2 *I* / *My* name is Fadi.
3 How old are *you* / *your*?
4 Is *you* / *your* class good?
5 Where's *he* / *him* from?
6 What time is *they* / *their* party?
7 How long is *we* / *our* class?
8 Who are *they* / *their*?
9 Here's *I* / *my* phone number. It's / He's 07490028.
10 *I* / *My* son's at university. *She's* / *He's* 21.
11 This is Maria. *She* / *Her* is in *we* / *our* English class.
12 *He* / *Her* husband is *I* / *my* boss.

NOT

I'm **not** from Moscow.	It's large – **not** small.
You're **not** 18.	It's 20 euros – **not** 30.
We're **not** from here.	He's 20 – **not** 16!
They're **not** new.	I'm from Manchester – **not** London.
It's **not** a black tea.	
He's **not** my husband.	
She's **not** a doctor.	

Exercise 1
Tick (✓) the correct sentence.
1 a My name's not Chelsea. ✓
   b Not my name's Chelsea.
2 a It's a large coffee – small not.
   b It's a large coffee – not small.
3 a I is not from New York.
   b I'm not from New York.
4 a How old you are?
   b How old are you?
5 a Where is she from?
   b Where she's from?
6 a I'm no Leo.
   b Are you Leo?
7 a He's her brother. Her name's Pedro.
   b He's her brother. His name's Pedro.
8 a They is not from here.
   b They're not from here.

PRONUNCIATION

Exercise 1
A ▶ 190 Listen and complete the questions. They're fast.
1 Who _____?
2 Where _____?
3 Where _____ from?
4 How much _____?
5 What day _____?
6 What _____?
7 How old _____?
8 What time _____?
9 How much _____?
10 How _____?
11 How old _____?
12 Where _____?
13 Who _____?
14 How long _____?

B ▶ 191 Listen again and check. They're slow.

2 LIVE, WORK, EAT

PRESENT SIMPLE
Verbs: (to) *live, know, like, have, take, work*

I	**live** near here.
You	**know** the city.
We	**like** it here.
They	**work** here.
My mother and father	**have** a nice house.
He	**live**s near here.
She	**know**s the city.
My brother	**like**s it here.
My friend Karen	**ha**s a nice flat.
It	
The bus	**take**s 10 minutes.

Exercise 1
Choose the correct word.
1 I *live* / *lives* in a flat.
2 My mother and father *live* / *lives* near me.
3 My friend Ali *have* / *has* a nice flat.
4 You *know* / *knows* the park. He *live* / *lives* near there.
5 I *know* / *knows* your sister. She *work* / *works* in the university, right?
6 We *walk* / *walks* to school. It *take* / *takes* an hour.
7 My wife *like* / *likes* Moscow, but I *like* / *likes* St Petersburg.
8 My family *live* / *lives* in a small village. We *know* / *knows* everyone in the village!

PRESENT SIMPLE QUESTIONS: *DO YOU ...?*

Where		live?
Who	**do you**	live with?
What time		go to work?
	Do you	live near here?
		know it?
		like it?

Exercise 1

A Write *do you* in the right places in the conversation. There are one or two in each part 1–5.

1 A: Where ^(do you) live?
   B: In Beppu. know it?
2 A: No. Where is it?
   B: It's a small city in the south of Japan.
   A: like it?
3 B: Yes. It's a nice place. Where live?
   A: Birmingham. know it?
   B: Yes. My friend lives there!
4 A: What's his name?
   B: Bryan.
   A: know his family name?
5 B: No. Sorry. like Birmingham?
   A: Yes, it's OK.

B ▶ 192 Listen and check.

be or do?

Be	Other verbs
Where **are you** from?	Where **do you** live?
How **are you**?	What **do you** do?
Are you OK?	**Do you** have a sister?
Are you married?	**Do you** know it?

Exercise 2
Complete the questions with *are* or *do*.
1 Where _____ you from?
2 What _____ you do?
3 How old _____ your children?
4 Who _____ you?
5 Where _____ you live? Is it near?
6 _____ you have a brother?
7 _____ you OK?
8 _____ you know my friend, Sara?
9 Where _____ you work?

Exercise 3
Match the answers (a–i) with the questions in Exercise 2.
a I'm a teacher.
b France.
c Five and seven.
d I'm fine, thanks.
e Yes, he's sixteen.
f Not far. I have a flat in Little Street.
g In an office.
h No. Nice to meet you.
i My name's Alex. I work here.

Exercise 4
Tick (✓) the correct question (a or b).
1 a Do you like it? ✓
   b You like?
2 a Are you live near here?
   b Do you live near here?
3 a Do it far?
   b Is it far?
4 a How are you?
   b How do you?
5 a Where you from?
   b Where are you from?
6 a What do you?
   b What do you do?

PRESENT SIMPLE: DON'T (DO NOT)
Negative forms

I **work** 50 hours a week.	I **don't work** here.
I **walk** to work.	I **don't walk** to work.
You **like** the area.	You **don't like** the area.
We **have** a house.	We **don't have** a house.
They **have** a big car.	They **don't have** a car.

Exercise 1
Choose the correct word(s).
1 I *like / don't like* my job. It's good.
2 I *like / don't like* meat. It's bad.
3 I *work / don't work*. I'm at school.
4 I *work / don't work*. I'm retired.
5 I *work / don't work* in a hospital. I'm a nurse.
6 I *have / don't have* a paid job. I'm at home with my son. He's two.
7 I *have / don't have* children. One daughter and one son.
8 I *have / don't have* a car. I take the bus.

Yes/No questions and short answers

Questions		Short answers	
		+	−
Do	I / you / they / Jia and Fan	**have** time for a coffee? **live** here? **like** fish? **work**?	Yes, you **do**. Yes, I **do**. Yes, they **do**. Yes, they **do**.	No, you **don't**. No, I **don't**. No, they **don't**. No, they **don't**.

Exercise 2
Write a short answer.
1 Do we have something to eat? (−)
   No, we don't.
2 Do you know her sister? (−)
3 Do you live near Bob? (+)
4 Do they like London? (+)
5 Do you have a car? (−)
6 Do we have time for a coffee? (+)
7 Do your children live with you? (−)

PLURAL / NO PLURAL
Plurals

Regular	
singular	plural (+ -s)
a daughter	two daughter**s**
a nurse	five nurse**s**
a flat	a lot of flat**s**
a boy	some boy**s**
a bus	two bus**es**
a city	some cit**ies**

Irregular	
singular	plural (no -s)
child	child**ren**
person	**people**
man	**men**
woman	**women**

Grammar reference 63

Exercise 1
Write the correct word in each sentence.

1 **job / jobs**
   a I have a good _____. I like it.
   b My brother works a lot. He has three _____.
2 **son / sons**
   a I have three _____ and a daughter.
   b My _____ is a nurse.
3 **teacher / teachers**
   a I'm a _____ in a university.
   b It's a big school with eighty _____.
4 **person / people**
   a Sixty _____ work at my company.
   b She's a nice _____.
5 **flat / flats**
   a We have two _____. One in the city and one in a village.
   b Our _____ is near here.
6 **woman / women**
   a All the English teachers in my school are _____!
   b Francisca is a great _____. She's a good friend.

No Plural

money	The money *is* good.
work	I do **a lot of** work.
meat	The meat *is* nice.
time	I don't have time.

Exercise 2
Tick (✓) the correct sentences.

1 a The hours are bad. ✓
   b The hours is bad.
2 a I eat a lot of meats.
   b I eat a lot of meat.
3 a I have some money.
   b I have some moneys.
4 a The people at work is nice.
   b The people at work are nice.
5 a My children is sixteen.
   b My child is sixteen.
6 a I don't like my works.
   b I don't like my work.
7 a Most people in the office are men.
   b Most people in the office are man.

Exercise 3
Write plurals. Two words have no plural.

1 a village / some small _____
2 a block of flats / lots of _____ of flats
3 one green salad / three green _____
4 one brother and one sister / two _____ and three _____
5 fruit / lots of _____
6 a shop / lots of _____
7 a kebab / two _____
8 a job / lots of _____
9 one room / five _____
10 wine / some _____
11 a chicken curry / two chicken _____

LIKE / DON'T LIKE

PLURAL WORDS		**NO PLURAL**	
I (don't) like them		*I (don't) like it*	
burgers		meat	rice
chips		chicken	bread
oranges		fish	fruit
apples		sugar	cheese
cakes		tea	coffee
pizzas		wine	beer
people		money	work
children			

Exercise 1
Write the correct sentences.

(😃) = I love it/them   (🙁) = I don't like it/them
(🙂) = I like it/them

1 oranges (😃) *I love them.*   6 cheese (🙂)
2 chicken (🙁) *I don't like it.*   7 pizzas (🙂)
3 coffee (🙁)   8 wine (🙁)
4 burgers (🙁)   9 work (🙂)
5 chips (🙂)   10 children (😃)

PRONUNCIATION

Exercise 1

A ▶ 193 Listen to these words. They are fast then slow.

1 do you
2 are you

B ▶ 194 Listen and choose the words you hear (a or b).

1   a do you   b are you
2   a do you   b are you
3   a do you   b are you
4   a do you   b are you
5   a do you   b are you
6   a do you   b are you
7   a Are you OK?   b Where do you work?
8   a Where are you from? b Where do you live?
9   a When are you here? b When do you work?
10 a Are you from here? b Do you live here?
11 a Are you friends?   b Do you know him?
12 a How are you?   b How do you get there?

Exercise 2

▶ 195 Listen and write the five questions you hear.

3 LOVE, WANT, NEED

NEGATIVES WITH *BE*

am	
I'm hungry.	*I'm **not*** hungry.
are	
You're very good.	*You're **not*** very good.
We're in Spain.	*We're **not*** in Spain.
They're friends.	*They're **not*** friends.

is

He's well.	He's **not** well.
She's at school.	She's **not** at school today.
He's married.	He's **not** married.
It's very big.	It's **not** very big.
This **is** my class.	This **is not** my class.
My son **is** tired.	My son's **not** tired.
The room's cold.	The room's **not** cold.

Exercise 1
Tick (✓) the correct sentence (a or b).
1. a It's not very expensive. ✓
   b Not it's very expensive.
2. a This exercise not is difficult.
   b This exercise is not difficult.
3. a I not Russian.
   b I'm not Russian.
4. a We's not married.
   b We're not married.
5. a You're not old!
   b Your not old!
6. a My mum and dad are not here.
   b My mum and dad is not here.

Exercise 2
Complete the sentences with the negative form of *be*.
1. He _____ from America. He's from Canada.
2. You _____ in this class. Sorry.
3. They _____ married.
4. We _____ retired. We work.
5. I _____ Conrad. I'm Constan.
6. I want it – and it _____ very expensive.
7. Sorry. My brother _____ here today.
8. It _____ a big town. It has 12,000 people.
9. Grammar _____ difficult. It's easy.
10. I _____ in this hotel. It's very expensive!

be: contractions

We also sometimes say *be* negatives in these ways:
You **aren't**	= You're **not**
We **aren't**	= We're **not**
They **aren't**	= They're **not**
It **isn't**	= It's **not**
He **isn't**	= He's **not**
She **isn't**	= She's **not**

He **isn't** from America. He's from Canada.
You **aren't** in this class. Sorry.

PRESENT SIMPLE: *DOESN'T*
Negative forms

Person	don't/doesn't	Verb
He She My brother Andrew	doesn't	**live** here. **work**. **have** any money. **like** it.
It	doesn't	**take** long.
I You We They	don't	**live** here. **work**. **have** any money. **like** it.

don't = do not; **doesn't** = does not

Exercise 1
Make the sentences negative.
1. I like fish. *I don't like fish.*
2. My son likes meat.
3. It takes a long time.
4. My mum and dad have a big house.
5. My friend Mikel has a very good job.
6. She lives near here.
7. We like this city.
8. I have money.

PRESENT SIMPLE QUESTIONS: *DOES*

Question word	does	person	verb
What Where Who How long What time	does	he she Ali it your wife	**do**? **work**? **live** with? **take**? **get** home?
	Does	it he your sister	**take** a long time? **live** here? **have** a car?

Exercise 1
Add *do*, *don't*, *does* or *doesn't* in the correct part of the conversations. You need one or two in each conversation.
1. A: I'm sorry, I know your name.
   I'm sorry, I don't know your name.
   B: Andrea.
2. A: you know this area?
   B: No. I live here.
3. A: What your mother do?
   B: She work now. She's retired.
4. A: Where Maria live?
   B: I know. Ask Simon. He knows her well.
5. A: Where your girlfriend work?
   B: Sorrento.
   A: How long it take to get there?
   B: Twenty or thirty minutes.

be or *do*?

be + adjective/noun	*do* + verb
I'm not **hungry**.	I don't **know**.
He's not **English**.	He doesn't **work** now.
Are they **police**?	Do they **have** a car?
Is your father very **old**?	Does your mum **work**?

Exercise 2
Choose the correct word.
1. What *do / is / does* she eat for lunch?
2. What time *are / is / does* your bus?
3. Where *is / does / do* he live?
4. *Does / Is / Do* your boss married?
5. Where *do / does / are* you from?
6. My daughter *don't / isn't / doesn't* eat meat.
7. *Is / Does / Do* your father like his job?
8. She *work / works / is work* in a school.
9. Where *is / are / do* your parents live?
10. *Are / Is / Do* the people in your class nice?

Grammar reference 65

A and ANY

I **don't** have I **don't** need I **don't** want	a	charger. pen. brush. towel.
Do you have **Do** you need **Do** you want	any	pens? towels? other clothes? milk? money? toothpaste?
	anything (else)?	

Exercise 1
Complete the sentences with *a* or *any*.
1. I have _____ flight at seven tomorrow.
2. Do you want _____ rice?
3. I'm sorry. I don't have _____ time this week.
4. It's _____ good restaurant.
5. I don't have _____ friends here.
6. My father is _____ driver and my mother is _____ nurse.
7. Do you have _____ pens?
8. I work in _____ coffee shop. It's _____ nice job.
9. My mother works in _____ hospital.
10. Do you have _____ milk?

Use *an* before a vowel sound.
I want **an** ice cream.
An orange juice, please.
an English class

PRONUNCIATION

Exercise 1

A ▶ 196 Listen to the phrases. They are fast then slow.
1. does he
2. does she
3. does it

B ▶ 197 Listen and choose the sentence you hear (a or b).
1. a Where does he work?
   b Where do you work?
2. a What time does the shop open?
   b What time does your class start?
3. a Does your brother have a car?
   b Do you have a car?
4. a Does he live near here?
   b Is it near here?
5. a What does she do?
   b What does it do?
6. a Do you know everyone?
   b Does she know your mum?
7. a Does he like it?
   b Does she like it?
8. a What does he know?
   b What does she know?

Exercise 2
▶ 198 Listen to the sentences. They are fast. Are they negative (–) or positive (+)?
1. __+__   5. ____   9. ____
2. __–__   6. ____ 10. ____
3. ____   7. ____ 11. ____
4. ____   8. ____ 12. ____

4 WHERE AND WHEN?

IS THERE ...? THERE'S ...

Is there a park near here?
Is there a bank near here?
There's one on this road.
There's a shop on the corner.

We use *is there .... ?* and *there's* with singular nouns.

Exercise 1
Complete the sentences with *is there* or *there's*.
1. A: I need to get some money. _____ a cash machine near here?
   B: Oh, right. _____ one in the bus station.
2. A: _____ a park near here?
   B: I'm sorry. I don't know the area.
3. A: Do you know a bar called Lisboa?
   B: No. _____ a place down there. I don't know its name.
4. A: _____ a supermarket near here?
   B: No, sorry, but _____ a fruit and vegetable shop on this road.
5. A: _____ a car park near here?
   B: Yes, _____ one next to the supermarket.
6. A: _____ a café near here?
   B: _____ one in the square. Go down there.

PREPOSITIONS AND DIRECTIONS

on

on the corner

down the road

in

next to

on the left

at the end

near

66

Exercise 1
Put the preposition in the correct place.

1 There's a small shop ^on^ the corner of this road. (on)
2 There's a restaurant the hotel. (in)
3 The hotel is the centre. (near)
4 The school is the main square. (in)
5 There's a nice café the school. (next to)
6 It's the next road. (on)
7 There's a swimming pool the park. (in)
8 There's a shop the next corner. (on)
9 There's a small park the end of our street. (at)
10 Is there a toilet the second floor? (on)
11 It's this road. Then take the second the right. (down / on)

Exercise 2
Put the words in the correct order.

1 near / a / here / supermarket / there / is / ?
Is there a supermarket near here?
2 road / a / hotel / on / this / there's / .
3 a / shop / there's / near / the / train / station / .
4 there / is / a / cash / here / near / machine / ?
5 one / there's / the / corner / on / .
6 near / is / swimming / pool / a / there / here / ?
7 at / there's / of / one / the / end / this / road / .

ADVERBS OF FREQUENCY

With be
The bank **is** <u>always</u> closed on Monday.
It**'s not** <u>normally</u> busy on Thursday.
He**'s** <u>often</u> late.
English **is** <u>sometimes</u> difficult.
I**'m** <u>never</u> late.
Are you <u>normally</u> free on Saturday?

With other verbs
Supermarkets <u>normally</u> **open** at 8 in the morning.
Children **don't** <u>usually</u> **have** classes at the weekend.
I <u>sometimes</u> **have** tea.
We **don't** <u>often</u> **have** coffee.
We <u>never</u> **work** on Friday.
Do you <u>normally</u> **work** late?

Exercise 1
Put the adverb in the correct place in each sentence.

1 I go out on Saturday night. (usually)
I usually go out on Saturday night.
2 They're late. (always)
3 I work on Saturday. (sometimes)
4 I go to mosque on Friday. (always)
5 I'm free on Wednesday afternoon. (normally)
6 I go swimming. (never)
7 We don't go out at night in the week. (usually)
8 I'm busy at the weekend. (never)
9 He's not here in the afternoon. (usually)
10 They go to the beach on Sunday morning. (sometimes)
11 I don't go to the cinema. (often)

Exercise 2
▶ 199 **Listen to the sentences. They are fast. Add the adverb you hear.**

1 I'm _____ late.
2 We _____ go to church on Sunday.
3 I'm not _____ busy on Thursday.
4 I _____ walk to work.
5 I _____ take the bus.
6 My wife _____ works in the evening.
7 My husband _____ has lunch at home.
8 My brother _____ takes my things.

CAN ...?
We use **can**/**can't** + verb.

Can I help you?	I **can** help.
	I **can't** help.
Can you help me?	You **can** help.
	You **can't** help.
Can he come tomorrow?	He **can** come.
	He **can't** come.
Can she speak English?	She **can** speak French.
	She **can't** speak English.
Can we do it now?	We **can** do it.
	We **can't** do it.
Can they wait?	They **can** wait.
	They **can't** wait.

Exercise 1
Complete the questions with the correct verb.

change   get   go   help   say   sit   wait   write

1 My English isn't good. Can you _____ it again slowly, please?
2 I have a big problem. Can you _____ me?
3 I don't know this word. Can you _____ it on the board?
4 Can you _____ one minute? I need to finish this.
5 I don't know how to get there. Can I _____ with you?
6 I don't have my book. Can I _____ next to you and share yours?
7 Can you _____ me a coffee? And I think Ben wants a tea.
8 This isn't chicken. It's fish. Can you _____ it, please?

Short answers
We sometimes say *can* / *can't* in the answers.

Can I open the window?
Of course you **can**.
Yes, you **can**.

Can I open the window?
I'm sorry, you **can't**.
No, you **can't**.

Grammar reference 67

Exercise 2
Complete the sentences with *can* or *can't*.
1. A: _____ you help me?
   B: Sorry, I _____ now. I'm busy.
2. A: It's difficult to hear. _____ you play it again?
   B: Of course I _____.
3. A: I don't feel well. _____ I leave early?
   B: Of course you _____.
4. A: I _____ see the board very well. _____ I sit at the front?
   B: Sorry, you _____. But I _____ turn on the light. Does that help?
   A: Yes, thanks.

Exercise 3
Write sentences with *can* and these words.
1. help me? (you)
   Can you help me?
2. hear you (I / not)
3. cook lots of different things (my mum)
4. speak English (they / not)
5. leave early (we)
6. write it on the board? (you)
7. come in now. (she)
8. help you? (I)
9. share a book? (you three)

PRONUNCIATION
Exercise 1
A ▶ 200 Listen to the words. They are fast then slow.
1. can
2. can't

B ▶ 201 Listen and choose the words you hear. They are fast.

	a	b
1	Sorry, I can.	Sorry, I can't.
2	You can.	You can't.
3	Can you?	Can't you?
4	I can see.	I can't see.
5	Can I use your phone?	Can't I use your phone?
6	You can sit here.	You can't sit here.
7	You can come in.	You can't come in.
8	I can play it again.	I can't play it again.
9	Can we leave now?	Can't we leave now?
10	He can use my tablet.	He can't use my tablet.
11	They can help you.	They can't help you.
12	Can you turn off the light?	Can't you turn off the light?

5 GOING PLACES

ARE THERE ...? / THERE ARE ...

There are + plural nouns

There are	fifteen some several a lot of no	shops on this street. nice restaurants in the village. people outside.
There aren't	any	nice places near here.
Are there	any	cafés near here? people outside?

Remember
People, *children*, *men* and *women* are plural!
There **are** always lots of **people** there.

With the singular, we use these forms:

There's ... + singular nouns

There's a/no train station in the village.
There isn't a restaurant in the hotel.
Is there a cinema near here?

There are no ... = there aren't any ...
There's no ... = there isn't a ...

Exercise 1
Make these sentences plural.
1. There's a man outside. *There are some men outside.*
2. There's no toilet. *There are no toilets.*
3. There's no bar near here.
4. There's a shop on this road.
5. There's a restaurant in the square.
6. There's no cinema in the area.
7. There isn't a hospital in the town.
8. There's one person in the café.
9. There's only one man in our class.

Exercise 2
Read the conversations with a hotel receptionist. Write one word in each space.

Conversation 1
A: Hello. Can I help you?
B: Yes. I want to have a walk. ¹_____ there any nice places near here?
A: There ²_____ a nice park down the road.
B: How do you get there?
A: It's best to take a bus. It takes ten minutes. There ³_____ four every hour.
B: Can I buy the ticket on the bus?
A: No. There's ⁴_____ machine next to the bus stop.

Conversation 2
A: Hi, I want to go into town. Are there ⁵_____ buses going there now?
B: Sorry. You need to drive – or take a taxi.
A: OK. Is there ⁶_____ taxi place near here?
B: No, but I can call one.
A: There ⁷_____ six people in our group.
B: OK. I can ask for two.
A: Thanks. How much is it normally?
B: Fifteen euros.
A: OK. ⁸_____ there a cash machine here?
B: Yes. There ⁹_____ one over there. Next to the toilets.
A: Oh yes. Thanks.

Short answers
We sometimes use short answers in replies to *Are there ...?*

Are there any good films at the cinema?
Yes, there **are**.
No, there **aren't**.

Exercise 3
Complete the conversations with short answers.
1. A: Are there any good places to eat here?
   B: No, _____. You need to go into the city.
2. A: Is there a hotel near here called the Grand View?
   B: Yes, _____. It's on the main road.
3. A: Is there a supermarket near here?
   B: No, _____, but there's a shop at the end of the road which sells fruit and vegetables and things.

TALKING ABOUT PLANS: *I'M/WE'RE GOING ...*

Plan	Where / What	When
I'm going We're going	home to a café to the shops to have lunch to meet my sister to see the game	now. this afternoon. at six. tonight. tomorrow. on Saturday. after the class.

Compare with the present simple for habits (*always, usually,* etc.):
I normally go home at five.
I go to mosque on Friday.
I often go to see my grandparents at the weekend.

Exercise 1
Complete with *am/ 'm, are/ 're* or *do*.
1. A: I _____ going to meet Joan later.
   B: Oh, OK. Say hello.
2. A: We _____ going to the shops. _____ you need anything?
   B: Can you buy some milk?
3. A: _____ you know Madrid?
   B: Not really. Why?
   A: I _____ going there at the weekend.
4. A: I _____ going home now.
   B: Really? _____ you OK?
   A: Yes. I _____ fine, but I need to do some work.
5. A: _____ you like football?
   B: Yes.
   A: We _____ going to see the game tonight. _____ you want to come?

Exercise 2
Sentences 1–8 are wrong. They need one more word. Write the correct sentence.
1. I going home at seven.
   I'm going home at seven.
2. We're going to the beach Saturday.
   We're going to the beach on Saturday.
3. Am going to the cinema tonight.
4. We're to have a coffee.
5. I'm going the park after the class.
6. We going to see the Old Town tomorrow.
7. We're going meet some friends later.
8. We're going to finish six.

Exercise 3
Choose the correct sentence (a or b).
1. a I normally go to the beach on Sundays.
   b I'm normally going to the beach on Sundays.
2. a I go to have lunch later.
   b I'm going to have lunch later.
3. a We're sometimes going to play tennis.
   b We're going to play tennis today.
4. a I go to the cinema a lot.
   b I go to the cinema tonight.
5. a We're going to have a walk now.
   b We have a walk now.

Other forms after *go*

I'm going We're going I need to go Do you want to go	shopp**ing** swimm**ing** runn**ing** for lunch for dinner for a walk for a run for a coffee	now. this afternoon. at six. tonight. tomorrow. on Saturday. after the class.

Exercise 4
▶ 202 **Listen and complete.**
1. Do you want to go for a _____?
2. I'm going _____ later.
3. I'm going for a _____. Do you want to come?
4. We're going _____ on Saturday.
5. Do you want to go out for _____ tonight?
6. I need to go for a _____.

ASKING ABOUT PLANS: *GOING* AND *DOING*

	Are you **going**?
What time Where	**are** you **going**?
What	**are** you **doing** after the class? **are** you **doing** tonight?

Compare with the present simple for *want*, *need* and habits.
What time do you need to be there?
Where do you want to go?
What do you do? (= *What's your job?* / *What do you normally do there?*)

Exercise 1
Choose the correct word(s).
1. A: What are you *do / doing* tonight?
   B: Nothing special. Why?
2. A: *Do / Are* you want to go for lunch with us?
   B: Sure. Where are you going?
3. A: I'm going to meet a friend later. Do you want to come?
   B: Where *are / do* you going?
4. A: I sometimes need to work late, but I like my job.
   B: What *do you do / are you doing*?
5. A: We're going out later – if you want to come.
   B: Where *do you go / are you going*?
6. A: *What time / Where* are you going to the party tonight?
   B: Ten o'clock.

Other questions

When		?
Why	**are you going**	?
Who		with?
How long		for?

Grammar reference **69**

Exercise 2

A Complete the conversations 1–6 with the answers a–e.

a Eight?
b My boyfriend.
c My company has an office there.
d Krakow – it's a city in Poland.
e Two weeks.
f I'm going to the dentist in the morning and I'm going to meet a friend at the airport in the afternoon.

1 A: I'm going to Qatar next week.
   B: Why are you going?
   A: _____
2 A: Do you want to go to the dinner together?
   B: Sure. What time?
   A: _____
3 A: We're going to Costa Rica on holiday.
   B: How long are you going for?
   A: _____
4 A: I'm sorry. I'm not free tomorrow.
   B: What are you doing?
   A: _____
5 A: I'm going to see *An American in Paris* tonight.
   B: Nice! Who are you going with?
   A: _____
6 A: I'm going away for the weekend.
   B: Where are you going?
   A: _____

B ▶ 203 Listen and check.

PRONUNCIATION

Exercise 1

A ▶ 204 Listen to the phrases. They are fast, then slow.

1 there are some
2 there's a
3 there aren't any
4 there isn't a
5 Are there any
6 Is there any

B ▶ 205 Listen and choose the words you hear (a or b).

1 a there are some
  b there's a
2 a there aren't any
  b there isn't a
3 a there's a
  b there isn't a
4 a there are some
  b there aren't any
5 a Are there any
  b Is there a
6 a Are there any good places to visit?
  b Is there a good place to eat?
7 a There aren't any shops near here.
  b There are some shops near here.
8 a There's no parking here.
  b There's some parking here.
9 a Is there a bus to the airport?
  b Are there any buses to the airport?
10 a There are two cash machines there.
   b There's a cash machine there.
11 a There's a shop at the end of the road.
   b There are shops at the end of the road.
12 a There's something in the back of the car.
   b There are some things in the back of the car.

6 AWAY FROM HOME

PAST SIMPLE: COMMON IRREGULAR VERBS

The verb **be** has two past forms – **was** and **were**.
ALL other verbs have only **one** past form.
The most common verbs – *be, have, go, do* – are all **irregular**. Learn them as words.

Person	Present	Past
I she/he/it	am is	**was**
you/we/they	are	**were**
I/you/we/they she/he/it	have has	**had**
I/you/we/they she/he/it	do does	**did**
I/you/we/they she/he/it	go goes	**went**

You can find a list of past forms for other verbs in *Outcomes Beginner* on page 74.

Past time words	
last night	yesterday
last Friday	yesterday morning
last week	yesterday afternoon
last year	

Exercise 1

Choose the correct word.

1 I *go / went* to the mountains last weekend.
2 I usually *have / had* lunch at one o'clock, but I don't have time today.
3 I *have / had* a lot of work last night. I *go / went* to bed late.
4 I love basketball. I often *go / went* to see a game.
5 We *are / were* from Brazil. And you?
6 Sorry I'm late. There *is / was* a problem at the airport.
7 A: How was your journey?
   B: It *is / was* fine, but I *am / was* tired now.
8 A: How are your parents?
   B: They *are / were* fine, thanks.
9 A: What do you do?
   B: Well, I *am / was* retired now, but I *am / was* a nurse.
10 A: What did you do yesterday?
   B: Not much. I *do / did* some work and I *go / went* to the gym.

Exercise 2

Complete the two sentences with the correct form of the verbs. One sentence is present, one sentence is past.

1 **be**
   a We __were__ at home all day yesterday.
   b My mum and dad __are__ from Morocco.
2 **go**
   a I usually _____ to my father's village at the weekend.
   b My wife _____ to Rome last week for business.
3 **do**
   a We _____ some shopping yesterday.
   b I usually _____ all my homework.

70

4 have
  a I _____ a very nice lunch with my family last Sunday.
  b My brother _____ a good job. The money's very good.
5 be
  a How _____ your hotel?
  b How _____ the film last night?

REGULAR PAST SIMPLE ENDINGS

Regular past simple forms end in **-ed**.

Present	Past
love(s)	I **loved** the film.
rain(s)	It **rained** a lot last week.
stay(s)	We **stayed** in a nice hotel.
share(s)	We **shared** a kitchen.
talk(s)	He **talked** a lot.
want(s)	She **wanted** to go out last night.
need(s)	They **needed** to do some work.

You can find a list of past forms for other verbs in *Outcomes Beginner* on page 74.

Exercise 1
Make these sentences past.
1 They talk a lot.
2 I need a coffee.
3 We share a flat.
4 It rains a lot in April.
5 She loves him.
6 I want to go.

Exercise 2
Complete the text with the past form of the verbs.
We ¹ _went_ (go) to the north of Spain on holiday. We ² _____ (want) to see the mountains. We ³ _____ (stay) in a small hotel in a village called Oubanca. We ⁴ _____ (have) a great view from our room. It ⁵ _____ (is) really beautiful. We ⁶ _____ (walk) in the area every day. It ⁷ _____ (rain) one or two times, but the weather ⁸ _____ (is) good. We ⁹ _____ (love) it. We want to go there again.

PAST SIMPLE NEGATIVES

Past negatives use a past form of *be* or *do*.
Compare the present and the past negatives.

Present	Past
Be	
There **isn't** anyone at the meeting.	There **wasn't** anyone at the meeting.
We **aren't** hungry.	We **weren't** hungry.
All other verbs	
I **don't** know.	I **didn't** know.
We **don't** go out a lot.	We **didn't** go out last night.
He **doesn't** have any money.	He **didn't** have any money.

Exercise 1
Choose the correct form.
1 I didn't like it. It *was / wasn't* very good.
2 The weather wasn't very good. It *rained / didn't rain* a lot.
3 We didn't see a lot. We *had / didn't have* time.
4 We didn't have a lot of money. We *stayed / didn't stay* in a cheap place.
5 I'm really hungry now. I *don't / didn't* have any breakfast this morning.
6 I didn't understand him. I *don't / didn't* speak Russian.

Exercise 2
Complete the sentences with the past simple negative or present simple negative of the verbs.
1 I _didn't go out_ yesterday. (go out)
2 I _____ last week. (work)
3 I'm going home. I _____ well. (feel)
4 We _____ usually _____ lunch at home. (have)
5 It took a long time to get here. We _____ the way. (know)
6 My mother _____ meat. She's a vegetarian. (eat)

PAST SIMPLE QUESTIONS

To make past questions with a verb use a past form of *do*.
Compare present and past questions.

Present	Past
Do you like it?	**Did you** like it?
What **do you** do?	What **did you** do last night?
Where **do you** live?	Where **did you** live before?
What time **do you** go home?	What time **did you** go home?

Exercise 1
Read the answers and complete the questions in the past simple or present simple.
1 A: What / do?
  B: I work for a technology company.
2 A: What / do last night?
  B: I had dinner with some friends.
3 A: Where / go after the class?
  B: We went shopping.
4 A: have a nice time on holiday?
  B: Yes, it was great, thanks.
5 A: Where / your parents live?
  B: With me! But they also have a house in a village near here.
6 A: What time / get up this morning?
  B: Five o'clock! That's why I'm so tired now!

Past simple questions with *be*

Present	Past
Where **are** you from?	Where **were** you yesterday?
How**'s** the hotel?	How **was** the hotel?
Is he OK?	**Was** he OK?
Are they happy?	**Were** they happy?

Grammar reference 71

Exercise 2
Complete the questions with the correct past simple form of *be*.

1 Where _____ you last week?
2 How _____ the party yesterday?
3 _____ there a lot of people there?
4 Why _____ they late?
5 How much _____ the tickets?
6 _____ it difficult to get there?

Exercise 3
Match the answers with the questions in Exercise 1.

a Great. The music was great and we danced a lot.
b There was a problem at the airport. Their flight was delayed.
c I was on holiday.
d They were free!
e No. We got a taxi from the airport.
f Not really. Fifteen or twenty.

Exercise 4
Read the answers and write full questions in the past simple.

1 A: What / do in St Petersburg?
   B: Lots of things. We went to see an opera one night.
2 A: What / see?
   B: Faust.
3 A: Good?
   B: Yes, it was.
4 A: Where / be?
   B: The Mariinsky Theatre.
5 A: How long / the opera?
   B: About three hours.
6 A: Sleep?
   B: No, I didn't! I saw all of it!

Short answers
We sometimes use short answers in replies.

A: **Did** you go out last night?	A: **Was** it a good tour?
B: Yes, I **did**.	B: Yes, it **was**.
B: No, I **didn't**.	B: No, it **wasn't**.

REVISION

Exercise 1
Look at the example. Find five more sentences that are wrong. Correct them.

1 Did you went to the museum? ✗ *Did you go to the museum?*
2 I went to see my brother in hospital yesterday. ✓
3 The hotel didn't had a nice restaurant.
4 There is a big problem at work last week.
5 Did you eat on the plane?
6 We go to the beach yesterday afternoon.
7 What you do yesterday evening?
8 We stayed in lots of nice places in Romania.
9 I not see you yesterday. Where were you?
10 How was your day?

PRONUNCIATION

Exercise 2
▶ 206 Listen to the sound of the regular past forms.

1 /d/ loved, rained, stayed, shared
2 /t/ talked
3 /ɪd/ wanted, needed

Exercise 3
▶ 207 Listen and repeat.

1 It rained a lot last week.
2 I stayed at home.
3 My brother talked to them.
4 I wanted to sleep.
5 I needed to eat something.
6 I shared a room with my sister.
7 I loved Costa Rica.

Exercise 4

A ▶ 208 Listen to the words. They are fast, then slow.

1 do you
2 did you

B ▶ 209 Listen and choose the words you hear (a or b).

1 a do you
  b did you
2 a do you
  b did you
3 a do you
  b did you
4 a do you
  b did you
5 a Do you know anyone here?
  b Did you know anyone there?
6 a Do you want a coffee?
  b Did you want a coffee?
7 a What do you do?
  b What did you do last night?
8 a What time do you go to bed?
  b What time did you go to bed?
9 a Do you live here?
  b Did you live there?
10 a Do you have any money?
   b Did you have any money?
11 a Where do you go?
   b Where did you go?
12 a Do you sleep well?
   b Did you sleep well?

VERB LIST AND VOCABULARY REFERENCE

REGULAR AND IRREGULAR VERBS

Present	Past simple	-ing form
add	added	adding
ask	asked	asking
be	was	being
become	became	becoming
break	broke	breaking
build	built	building
buy	bought	buying
can	could	–
change	changed	changing
choose	chose	choosing
come	came	coming
continue	continued	continuing
cost	cost	costing
cut	cut	cutting
die	died	dying
do	did	doing
drink	drank	drinking
drive	drove	driving
eat	ate	eating
feel	felt	feeling
find	found	finding
get	got	getting
give	gave	giving
go	went	going
grow	grew	growing
happen	happened	happening
have	had	having
hear	heard	hearing
help	helped	helping
hit	hit	hitting
hold	held	holding
hurt	hurt	hurting
keep	kept	keeping
know	knew	knowing
learn	learned or learnt	learning
leave	left	leaving
lend	lent	lending
like	liked	liking
live	lived	living
look	looked	looking
lose	lost	losing
love	loved	loving
make	made	making
mean	meant	meaning
meet	met	meeting

Present	Past simple	-ing form
move	moved	moving
need	needed	needing
offer	offered	offering
open	opened	opening
pay	paid	paying
play	played	playing
prefer	preferred	preferring
put	put	putting
read	read	reading
remember	remembered	remembering
run	ran	running
see	saw	seeing
sell	sold	selling
send	sent	sending
show	showed	showing
sing	sang	singing
sit	sat	sitting
sleep	slept	sleeping
speak	spoke	speaking
spend	spent	spending
stand	stood	standing
start	started	starting
stay	stayed	staying
stop	stopped	stopping
study	studied	studying
swim	swam	swimming
take	took	taking
talk	talked	talking
teach	taught	teaching
tell	told	telling
think	thought	thinking
throw	threw	throwing
travel	travelled	travelling
try	tried	trying
turn	turned	turning
understand	understood	understanding
use	used	using
wait	waited	waiting
walk	walked	walking
want	wanted	wanting
watch	watched	watching
wear	wore	wearing
win	won	winning
work	worked	working
write	wrote	writing

Red words are in the list of 100 most frequent verbs in English.

VOCABULARY REFERENCE

COUNTRIES AND COUNTRY ADJECTIVES

Country	Country adjective	Capital
Argen**tina**	Argen**tin**ian	Buenos Aires
Bra**zil**	Bra**zil**ian	Brasília
Chile	**Chi**lean	Santiago
China	**Chi**nese	Beijing
Co**lom**bia	Co**lom**bian	Bogotá
France	**French**	Paris
Italy	**It**alian	Rome
Ja**pan**	Japa**nese**	Tokyo
Mexico	**Me**xican	Mexico City
Mo**ro**cco	Mo**ro**ccan	Rabat
Pe**ru**	Pe**ru**vian	Lima
Poland	**Po**lish	Warsaw
Russia	**Ru**ssian	Moscow
Saudi Arabia	**Sau**di	Riyadh
South Ko**rea**	Ko**rea**n	Seoul
Spain	**Spa**nish	Madrid
Thailand	**Thai**	Bangkok
The **UK**	**Brit**ish	London
The U**S** / The **States**	A**me**rican	Washington D.C.
Viet**nam**	Vietna**mese**	Hanoi

COLOURS

- black
- blue
- brown
- green
- grey
- pink
- **o**range
- **pur**ple
- red
- white
- **yel**low
- **dark** blue
- **light** blue

DATES

Months
January
February
March
April
May
June
July
August
Sep**tem**ber
Oc**to**ber
No**vem**ber
De**cem**ber

Monday	Tuesday	Wednesday	Thursday	Friday	Saturday	Sunday
1 the first	2 the second	3 the third	4 the fourth	5 the fifth	6 the sixth	7 the seventh
8 the eighth	9 the ninth	10 the tenth	11 the eleventh	12 the twelfth	13 the thirteenth	14 the fourteenth
15 the fifteenth	16 the sixteenth	17 the seventeenth	18 the eighteenth	19 the nineteenth	20 the twentieth	21 the twenty-first
22 the twenty-second	23 the twenty-third	24 the twenty-fourth	25 the twenty-fifth	26 the twenty-sixth	27 the twenty-seventh	28 the twenty-eighth
29 the twenty-ninth	30 the thirtieth	31 the thirty-first				

YEARS

1850	eighteen fifty	1901	nineteen oh one	1700	seventeen hundred
1800–1899	the 19th Century	2000–2099	the 21st Century	1900	nineteen hundred
1993	nineteen ninety-three	2005	two thousand and five	2000	the year two thousand
1900–1999	the 20th Century	2010	twenty ten		

Vocabulary reference 75

PRONOUNS

		Person	Thing	Place
		who	what which	where
every / all		**ev**erybody **ev**eryone	**ev**erything	**ev**erywhere
no / none		**no**body **no**-one	**no**thing	**no**where
any		**any**body **any**one	**any**thing	**any**where
a *or* an (one not specific)		**some**body **some**one	**some**thing	**some**where
the (specific)		he, she, etc. him, her, etc.	it one/ones	
near			this/these	here
far			that/those	there

LETTERS AND SOUNDS

Consonant sounds

Letter(s)	Most common sound → less common		
B b	/b/ baby husband brother bad	silent lamb	
C c	/k/ coffee doctor o'clock cut	/s/ city price juice nice	
Ch ch	/tʃ/ lunch teacher children choose	/k/ school	

Letter(s)	Most common sound → less common		
D d	/d/ don't drink food student	/t/ asked talked	
F f	/f/ father flat fifty wife	/v/ of	
G g	/g/ good give big English	/ŋ/ long anything listening reading	/dʒ/ orange page large village

Letter(s)	Most common sound → less common		
gh	silent right daughter eighty high		
H h	/h/ hi have how husband		
J j	/dʒ/ job juice Japan		
K k	/k/ drink milk take kitchen	silent know knew	
L l	/l/ like listen flat village	/əl/ people single table	
M m	/m/ meet I'm milk mum		
N n	/n/ in new not seventy	/ŋ/ ring long reading working	
P p	/p/ page people repeat map		
Ph ph	/f/ photo phone		
Qu qu	/kw/ question quite quiet square		

Letter(s)	Most common sound → less common		
R r	/r/ right red drink sorry		
S s	/s/ seven listen class cakes	/z/ is was plays	/ʃ/ discussion
Sh sh	/ʃ/ she shop fresh English		
T t	/t/ time tea twenty hot	/ʃ/ station action national dictionary	silent listen castle soft drink don't know
Th th	/ð/ the that's mother with	/θ/ three thanks sixteenth south	
V v	/v/ five have never very		
W w	/w/ we with twelve flower	silent two answer	
Wh wh	/w/ what when why white	/h/ who whole	
X x	/ks/ six taxi expensive next		
Y y	/j/ yes you your yellow		

Vowel sounds

Letter(s)	Most common sound → less common						
	/æ/	/eɪ/	/ə/	/e/	/ɔː/	/ɒ/	/ɑː/
A a	black have that can	same plane station conversation	a again abroad another	any anything many	water always talk	want	can't
	/eɪ/	/eə/	/e/	/ɪ/			
ai	email waiter train wait	pair air fair	again said	mountain			
	/eɪ/	/e/					
ay	day play way	says					
	/ɑː/	/eə/					
ar	are large far	area care					
	/e/	silent	/ɪ/	/iː/	/ə/		
E e	ten help fresh very	five name talked played	English wanted decided chooses	he she people email	the listen		
	/iː/						
ee	three meet week see						
	/iː/	/eɪ/	/e/	/ɪə/			
ea	tea teacher leave please	break great	weather breakfast	idea area			
	/ɜː/	/ə/	/eə/				
er	person were verb	sister answer enter	there where				
	/ɪə/	/ɜː/	/eə/				
ear	near year	learn early	wear				
	/ɪ/	/aɪ/					
I i	is in six drink	I nine price right					
	/i/	/juː/	/e/				
ie	cities countries companies	view review	friend				
	/ə/						
io(n)	question dictionary station discussion						

Letter(s)	Most common sound → less common				
O o	/ɒ/ hot not conversation sorry	/əʊ/ both don't clothes cold	/ʌ/ brother does London son	/uː/ do to who	/ə/ do you to work
oo	/uː/ food too choose school	/ʊ/ good look book	/ɔː/ floor		
ou	/aʊ/ house south about mountain	/uː/ you group	/ʌ/ country	/ə/ famous continuous	/ʊ/ would could
oa	/əʊ/ road coat soap goal	/ɔː/ board abroad			
oi	/ɔɪ/ point toilet				
ow	/əʊ/ know show window own	/aʊ/ how now towel shower			
oy	/ɔɪ/ boy toy enjoy				
or	/ɔː/ more or for	/ə/ actor doctor for you	/ɜː/ work		
our	/ɔː/ four your tour	/aʊə/ hour	/ɑː/ our		
U u	/ʌ/ number bus husband lunch	/uː/ student university use	/ʊ/ full put	/ə/ medium	/ɪ/ minute
ui	/ɪ/ build building	/uː/ juice fruit			
uy	/aɪ/ buy				
y	/aɪ/ my try	/i/ very thirty city	/ɪ/ system		

Vocabulary reference 79

INFORMATION FILES

FILE 1

Unit 1 pages 8 and 9   DEVELOPING CONVERSATIONS

FILE 2

Unit 1 page 12   VOCABULARY

Student B

Ask the prices. Complete the menu.

MENU

	Large	Medium	Small
Hot drinks			
cappuccino	_____	3.40	2.90
latte	3.75	3.40	2.90
americano	3.10	_____	_____
espresso	2.05	_____	
tea	2.25	1.95	1.60
Cold drinks			
fresh orange juice	4.35	3.95	3.45
Coke	_____		
water	1.35		
Food			
cakes	_____	sandwiches	6.50

FILE 3

Unit 4 page 35   GRAMMAR

Student A

A

FILE 4

Unit 4 page 35 GRAMMAR

Student B

AUDIO SCRIPTS, UNITS 1-6

AUDIO SCRIPTS

UNIT 1

▶ TRACK 6

B = Bob, T = Tina, P = Poppy, C = Connor
1 B: Tina is my wife. She's a doctor. This is my daughter, Poppy and he is my son Connor.
2 T: Bob is my husband. He's a teacher in an English school.
3 P: My mother is a doctor and my father is a teacher. Connor is my big brother.
4 C: Poppy's my sister. She's eight. Kevin is my best friend. We're in the same class at school.

▶ TRACK 8

1 A: Who is Maria?
   B: She's my wife.
2 A: Who is he?
   B: Greg. He's our teacher.
3 A: Lara. This is my sister, Katia.
   B: Hi. Nice to meet you.
4 A: You're Ana, right?
   B: No. I'm Zeynep. She's Ana!
   A: Oh! Sorry!
5 A Who are they?
   B: They're my children!
   A: Nice! What are their names?
   B: My son is Cristiano and my daughter is Inés.

▶ TRACK 9

1
A: He's my friend, Peter.
2
A: Who's she?
B: My mother.
3
A: What's her name?
B: Fatima.

▶ TRACK 11

1 ten, twelve, fourteen, sixteen
2 four, eight, twelve, sixteen
3 seven, eleven, thirteen, seventeen
4 one, three, six, ten

▶ TRACK 12

1 ten, twelve, fourteen, sixteen, eighteen
2 four, eight, twelve, sixteen, twenty
3 seven, eleven, thirteen, seventeen, nineteen
4 one, three, six, ten, fifteen

▶ TRACK 14

1 Who is she?
2 Where is it?
3 What time is it?
4 How much is it?
5 How long is it?
6 How old is she?

▶ TRACK 15

1 A: How are you?
   B: Fine, thanks.
2 A: How long is the class?
   B: One hour.
3 A: How old are you?
   B: Thirteen.
4 A: Where are you from?
   B: China.
5 A: Who's she?
   B: My mother.
6 A: How much is lunch?
   B: Sixteen dollars.
7 A: What time is it?
   B: Three o'clock.
8 A: What's your phone number?
   B: 0694 55 781.

▶ TRACK 16

1 Where are you from?
2 How are you?
3 Where is he from?
4 How long is the class?
5 How old are you?
6 What time is the party?
7 How old is your son?
8 Is she nice?
9 Who is he?
10 How much is it?

▶ TRACK 19

1
A: What time is it?
B: Three thirty-five.
2
A: How much is it?
B: It's fifteen seventy.
3
A: What time is the class?
B: Eleven o'clock.
4
A: What time is the coffee break?
B: Twelve fifteen.
5
A: How much is a cappuccino?
B: Four euros eighty.
6
A: What time is lunch?
B: One thirty.
7
A: How much are the sandwiches?
B: Eight ninety-five.
8
A: What time's your bus?
B: Sixteen fifty-two.

84

▶ TRACK 21
1 a large cappuccino
2 a medium latte
3 a small orange juice
4 a medium tea
5 a large americano
6 How much is a medium cappuccino?
7 How much are sandwiches?
8 How much is a large orange juice?

▶ TRACK 23
A: Yes sir. How are you today?
B: Er, yes, good.
A: What would you like?
B: Er, two coffees – large.
A: Cappuccino? Latte? Americano?
B: Er, one cappuccino and one americano with milk.
A: OK. Americano – with milk. Anything else?
B: Yes. One medium tea.
A: Milk?
B: No. No milk, thanks. And a juice for my daughter.
A: OK. Is that large?
B: No – small.
A: OK. One large cappuccino. One large americano with milk, one medium black tea, one small orange juice. Anything else?
B: And two of those. What's that?
A: Chocolate cake?
B: Yes, please. Two.
A: OK. And two chocolate cakes. That's twenty-two fifteen.
B: Sorry. How much?
A: Twenty-two pounds fifteen pence.
B: Is fifty OK?
A: Yes. Your change. Next.

▶ TRACK 24
A: That's twenty-two fifteen.
B: Sorry. How much?
A: Twenty-two pounds fifteen pence.
B: Is fifty OK?
A: Yes. Your change. Next. Are you OK?
B: Er, it's not right.
A: Sorry. What's the problem?
B: The change. This is seventeen eighty five.
A: Yeah.
B: Seventeen's not right. Twenty-two fifteen and seventeen eighty-five – that's not fifty pounds.
A: Oh yes. You're right. Sorry. Sorry. Here's ten more.
B: OK. Thank you.

▶ TRACKS 25 & 26
1 A: What's the problem?
   B: My tea – it's not right.
2 A: What's the problem?
   B: My coffee. It's not a cappuccino.
3 A: Yes. Sir. Are you OK?
   B: Sorry. It's a small tea – not large.
4 A: Are you OK?
   B: No. It's coffee cake – not chocolate.
5 A: Is everything OK?
   B: No. My tea's not hot.
6 A: What's the problem?
   B: It's not right. It's not 35 euros. It's 29.

▶ TRACKS 27 & 28
1 What's her name?
2 This is my friend, Don.
3 This is my son, John.
4 What time is the class?
5 Where are you from?
6 What's your phone number?

UNIT 2

▶ TRACK 33
My name's Leo.
I'm from Chile.
I live in a city called Temuco.
Temuco is in an area called Araucanía. It's in the south of Chile.
I live in a small house with my daughter and my dog.
It's on Los Leones road.
It's near the university.

▶ TRACKS 34 & 35
1 A: Where do you live?
   B: London.
2 A: Do you live with your brother?
   B: No. I live with a friend.
3 A: Who do you live with?
   B: My husband and my dog!
4 A: Do you like your city?
   B: Yeah. It's OK.
5 A: Do you know my name?
   B: Yes – it's Mohammed.
6 A: Do you have a house or a flat?
   B: A house.

▶ TRACK 36
A: Hi. Sorry. What's your name?
B: Ali. And you?
A: Maria. Nice to meet you.
B: You too.
A: So, Ali. Where do you live?
B: Clayton. It's a small village. Do you know it?
A: No. Is it far?
B: It takes thirty minutes by car. And you? Where do you live?
A: I live on Havana Road. Do you know it?
B: Yes. It's near here, right?
A: Yes. I walk here. It takes fifteen minutes.

▶ TRACK 37
A: Hi. Sorry. What's your name?
B: Otar. And you?
A: Tamar. Nice to meet you.
B: You too. Where do you live?
A: District 7. And you?
B: I live in District 3.
A: I know it. It's near.
B: Yes. I walk here.

Audio scripts 85

TRACK 39

1
A: What do you do?
B: I'm a bus driver.
2
A: What do you do?
B: I'm a teacher in a language school.
3
A: What do you do?
B: I'm a waiter.
4
A: What do you do?
B: I'm a student. I'm at university.
5
A: What do you do?
B: I'm a nurse.
6
A: What do you do?
B: I work in an office.
7
A: What do you do?
B: I don't have a job. I'm retired.
8
A: What do you do?
B: I'm a mum. I don't work for money.

TRACK 40

1 I don't work on Friday and Saturday.
2 I don't know.
3 You don't live near here.
4 I don't like it.
5 We don't have children.
6 They don't live in the centre.
7 I don't walk to class.
8 I don't go to a language school.

TRACK 42

My name's Carlos. I'm from Mexico, but now I live in London. I live in north London and I work in a university in the south. It takes 80 minutes by train. The job's great. I like my students and the money's OK.

TRACK 43

1
My name's Jessica. I'm from Australia, but I'm a nurse here in London. My job's OK, but I don't like the hospital. It's small and I don't live near it. It's an hour by car from my flat. The other nurses are nice, but I don't like some doctors.
2
My name's Rasa. I'm from Lithuania, but now I live and work in Tooting – an area in south London. I work in an office. It's OK. I like the people and the hours are good for me. I work from nine to three and then I go to a language school.
3
My name's Ali. I'm from Turkey. I work for a taxi company. I don't like my job. London traffic is bad. The money is OK but I work a lot – 70 or 80 hours a week. I don't have time with my wife and two daughters.

TRACK 44

A: What do you do?
B: I'm a taxi driver.
A: Do you like it?
B: No.
A: Why not?
B: The hours are bad.

TRACK 47

A: Do you have a table for three?
B: Yes. Would you like a menu in English?
A: Please.
B: Would you like some drinks?
A: Yes. Two orange juices, a Coke and some water.

TRACK 48

B: Are you ready to order?
A: Yes. A kebab with rice for me.
B: And for you?
C: Chicken, please.
B: With rice or chips?
C: Chips, please.
B: And you?
D: Prawns with rice.
B: Anything else? A salad?
C: How much is the tomato salad?
B: Fifteen euros.
C: Oh. It's expensive. No, thanks.

TRACK 49

A: Do you have a table for three?
B: Yes. Would you like a menu in English?
B: Please.
A: Would you like some drinks?
B: Yes. Two orange juices, a Coke and some water.
B: Are you ready to order?
A: Yes. A kebab with rice for me.
B: OK. And you?
C: Chicken, please.
B: With rice or chips?
C: Chips, please.
B: And you?
D: Prawns with rice.
B: Anything else? A salad?
C: How much is the tomato salad?
B: Fifteen euros.
C: Oh. It's expensive. No, thanks.
B: So, that's one kebab and rice, one chicken and chips and one prawns with rice.

TRACKS 50 & 51

1 It's a nice area.
2 It's in the north.
3 She's a teacher in a language school.
4 Where do you live?
5 I like it here.
6 I don't live near here.
7 I don't know it.
8 I don't like it.
9 He's a student at university
10 They have a nice house.

UNIT 3

▶ TRACK 55

1
A: How's your room?
B: It's not very big. How's *your* room?
A: The same. And it's old!
B: Yeah, I know.
2
A: How's the class?
B: It's good, but English is difficult.
A: Yes!
3
A: How's the chicken?
B: It's not very nice.
A: Oh no! I'm sorry.
B: How's the fish?
A: It's great!
B: Good.
4
A: How's the weather?
B: It's cold. It's not good.
A: Oh no! It's normally hot there.

▶ TRACK 56

1 She's not my friend.
2 It's not a big city.
3 We're not married.
4 I'm not very hungry.
5 They're not from here.
6 The rooms are not very expensive.
7 My job's not very good. The money's not great.

▶ TRACK 58

1 A: It's not very expensive.
   B: Oh, good.
2 A: My room is nice and big.
   B: Oh, good.
3 A: It's very cold in my flat.
   B: I'm sorry.
4 A: The weather here is great.
   B: Oh, good.
5 A: I love my English class.
   B: Oh, good.
6 A: The fish is very good.
   B: Oh, good.
7 A: My father's not very well.
   B: I'm sorry.
8 A: I don't like my new job. The hours are very bad.
   B: I'm sorry.

▶ TRACK 59

A: How's your room?
B: Very nice. It's big.
A: Oh, good. How's the restaurant?
B: It's not very good. It's expensive.

▶ TRACK 60

1 take the bus
   take a photo
   take a shower
   take a long time
2 go to the park every day
   go to the doctor
   go on holiday
   go shopping
3 want a coffee
   want a new house
   want to go to China
   want to buy some clothes

▶ TRACK 63

J = Janet, W = Wilton, A = Aled, B = Ben
J: Hello. Are you Wilton?
W: Yes, yes.
J: Hi. Nice to meet you! I'm Janet.
W: Hello. Janet. Nice to meet you too.
J: Come in. Leave your bag there.
W: OK, thanks.
J: Come in. Meet my family.
W: Yes, thank you.
J: So Wilton is a student and he's with us for one month.
A/B: Welcome. Hi.
J: These are my sons Aled and Ben.
W: Ben and … can you say that again?
A: Aled.
W: Nice to meet you.
A: Yeah, you too. How are you?
W: Good, thanks.
J: You're not tired?
W: No. I'm OK.
B: Where are you from, Wilton?
W: Arequipa.
B: Sorry – where?
W: Arequipa – Peru.

▶ TRACK 64

B: Where are you from, Wilton?
W: Arequipa.
B: Sorry – where?
W: Arequipa – Peru.
B: OK. How long does it take to get here?
W: Sorry. Can you say it again?
B: How long does it take from Peru to here?
W: Oh, er, sixteen hours.
A: OK. A long time! But you're not tired.
W: No. I … I'm OK.
J: Are you hungry? Do you want anything to eat?
W: Sorry. Can you say that again?
J: Yeah sorry. Are you hungry? … Do you want any food?
W: Er. No. Thank you. Do you have any tea?
J: Of course. Do you want any milk in it?
W: Sorry?
J: Tea with milk?
W: No – black. Thanks.
J: And you don't want anything else? No food?
W: No, thank you. Er … do you have a … for my phone?
J: A charger?

W: Yes. My phone doesn't have … er, *batería*. How do you say it?
A: It's the same – battery!
W: Yes, my phone has no battery and I need a …can you say it?
A: Charger!
W: Yes, I don't have my charger. It's in Peru!
J: Oh, OK. Ben, do you have a charger?
B: What phone is it?
W: This.
B: Oh yes – no problem.

▶ TRACK 65

A: How are you?
B: Sorry? Can you say that again?
A: How are you?
B: Oh, I have … how do you say *tengo hambre*?
A: I'm hungry.
B: Yes. I'm hungry.
A: Do you want a sandwich?
B: Yes, please.

▶ TRACK 66

Sorry? Can you say that again?
How do you say *batería* (in English)?

▶ TRACK 67

1 A: Do you need a dictionary?
　B: No, thanks. I understand the word.
2 A: Do you have any money? I only have euros.
　B: Yes. How much do you need?
3 A: It's very cold here. Do you have any other clothes?
　B: Yes. I have a big coat.
4 A: Do you need a towel?
　B: No, it's OK. I have one.
5 A: Do you want any food?
　B: Yes, please. I'm hungry.
6 A: Do you have any brothers or sisters?
　B: Yes. One brother and three sisters.

▶ TRACKS 68 & 69

1 Do you have a pen?
2 Do you have any brothers or sisters?
3 Do you want to go shopping?
4 I don't have a lot of free time.
5 How's your class?
6 It's not very nice. It's very cold.
7 How's the weather?
8 It's not very expensive.

UNIT 4

▶ TRACKS 72 & 73

1 Is there a café near here?
　Yes. There's one on this road. Down there. On the left.
2 Is there a supermarket near here?
　Yes. There's one next to the train station.
3 Is there a bank near here?
　Yes. There's a Santander bank on this road. Down there. On the right.
4 Is there a hospital near here?
　Sorry. I don't know. I don't live here.

▶ TRACK 74

1
A: Hi. Excuse me. Excuse me!
B: Sorry. Yes.
A: Is there a cash machine near here?
B: A cash machine … er… yeah. There's one down there.
A: How far is it?
B: I don't know – 200 metres? It's next to a small supermarket called Jones.
A: OK – next to the supermarket.
B: Yeah – it's on the left. The other side of the road.
A: Oh, OK! Thanks.
2
A: Excuse me. Do you know a restaurant called Gema near here?
B: Er … I don't know. I don't know the area.
A: Oh.
B: There are some restaurants on this road, but I don't know their names.
A: Oh, OK.
B: Go down this road. I think the first one is a pizza place.
A: Oh yes – pizza! It's a pizza restaurant.
B: Maybe that's it. Down here on the right.
A: OK. Thank you!
3
A: Excuse me. Hello.
B: Yes.
A: Is there a car park near here?
B: A car park … car park. Oh, wait, yes – there's one on London Road. Down here. The second on the right.
A: Sorry, can you say that again?
B: Sorry, yeah. So, down here. The second road. Go right.
A: The second road.
B: Yes. It's a big road called London Road. And on London Road the car park is on the left.
A: OK. Thank you.

▶ TRACK 75

1
A: Is there a swimming pool near here?
B: Yes. There's one on Green Road. It's next to the park.
A: OK, thanks.
2
A: Do you know a church called St Mary's?
B: Yes. It's on Church Road.
A: Is it far?
B: No. It's about ten minutes from here.

▶ TRACK 80

1
T = teacher, S = student
T: James. Are you OK?
S: No. It's difficult. Can you help me?
T: Sure.

2
T: Kevin. Are you OK?
S: Can you close the window? I'm cold.
T: Is everybody else cold?
S: Yes.
T: Oh, OK. Sure.

3
S1 = Student 1, S2 = Student 2
S1: Do you want to go and have a coffee?
S2: Sure. Can you wait a minute? I need to go to the toilet.
S1: OK.
S2: Where is it?
S1: Oh – it's on the second floor. Next to the stairs.

4
S: I'm sorry. I can't come to class on Thursday.
T: OK. Can you do exercises 6 and 7?
S: Sure.
T: And exercise 8.
S: OK.
T: And maybe read page 39.
S: It's a lot!

5
T: Are you OK?
S: We're tired. Can we have a break?
T: Of course. Sorry.
S: Is there a café near here?
T: Yes there's one on this road. On the right.
S: How long do we have?
T: Ten minutes.
S: Can we have drinks in the class?
T: No, sorry. You can't.
S: OK. Can we have five more minutes? We don't have time to drink our coffee.
T: Yes, fine.

▶ TRACKS 81 & 82

1 Do you know a town called Atrani?
2 Is there a hospital near here?
3 Are you free tomorrow night?
4 It's down this road on the right.
5 I normally work late on Mondays.
6 It's at the end of this road on the left.
7 There's one on the third floor.
8 There's one near here. The first road on the right.

▶ TRACK 83

1 Does she have any brothers or sisters?
2 I sometimes go shopping in the market near here.
3 They're not in my class at school.
4 Do you need anything else?
5 There's a car park on the left.

UNIT 5

▶ TRACKS 85 & 87

1
A: I want to buy some new clothes. Are there any good shops near here?
B: Yes. Try an area called Cihangir. I always go shopping there. There are lots of nice places.
A: OK. How do you get there?
B: Oh, you can walk. It's not very far. Maybe ten minutes.
A: Thank you.

2
C: I want to go swimming this afternoon. Where's the best place to go?
D: Well, there's a pool on this road. Or there's a beach about thirty minutes from here.
C: A beach is good. How do you get there?
D: Take the train. The station is two minutes from here. Leave the hotel. Go left. It's there. Trains go every fifteen minutes, so …
C: Great. Thank you.

3
E: Are there any places to go out in the evening here?
F: Not in the village. People go to the town. There's a cinema in the town and there are some nice places in the main square.
E: OK. How do you get there?
F: Car or taxi. It takes twenty minutes.
E: How much is a taxi?
F: About twenty euros.

4
G: Is there a nice café or restaurant near here? I want to have some lunch.
H: Yes. There are lots of good places. Try Ariel. It's on a street called Szeroka. In Kazimierz.
G: OK. Thank you. How do you get there?
H: Take the bus. Number 16 and number 25 go there. The stop is one minute from here.
G: Great. How long does it take?
H: About ten minutes.

5
I: Hello there. I want to see some interesting art today. Where's a good place to visit?
J: Well, there's a good museum in the centre. It's near the station.
I: OK. Thanks. How do you get there?
J: You can take the bus, but it's best to get a taxi. It takes ten or fifteen minutes. They're not very expensive.
I: OK. Thank you. Can I get a taxi from here?
J: Yes, of course. I can phone and get one for you.

▶ TRACK 88

A: Hello. Can I help you?
B: Yes I want to have a walk. Is there anywhere nice near here?
A: There's a nice park down the road.
B: How do you get there?
A: It's best to take a bus! It takes ten minutes. Or you can walk. It takes twenty minutes.
B: OK. Thanks.

Audio scripts 89

TRACK 91

A = assistant, T = tourist
A: Do you want to buy a ticket?
T: Er... yes.
A: You can use the machine over here. You can pay by cash or card and you don't need to wait.
T: Oh, OK. Is the machine in German?
A: Yes, but I can help you. Come with me.
T: OK.
A: Where are you going?
T: Lausanne.
A: Single or return?
T: Return.
A: For now, right?
T: Yes. And back on Monday.
A: Yes, fine. First class? Second class?
T: Second class is fine.
A: OK. Do you want a receipt?
T: Yes, please.
A: Put your card in here and enter your number.
T: OK.
A: And here are your tickets and receipt.
T: When's the next train?
A: 9.47. From platform eight.
T: Sorry. Which platform?
A: Eight — at 9.47.
T: OK. Thank you for your help.
A: You're welcome. Have a good day.

TRACK 92

1
A: What are you doing now?
B: I'm going home. I need to study. And you?
A: I'm going to have a coffee. Do you want to come?
B: Sorry, I can't. I don't have time today.
A: OK. See you tomorrow.

2
C: What are we doing now? Do you want to get something to eat?
D: No. I'm going to stay here.
C: Are you going to your room now?
D: Yes. I'm tired. I'm going to bed. It's an early flight tomorrow.
C: That's true. What time are we going?
D: Five. The flight is at 7.15 and it takes thirty minutes to the airport.
C: Right. Well, I need to eat something.
D: OK. I'll meet you here tomorrow morning.
C: Five o'clock?
D: That's right. See you then.
C: Yep. Sleep well.

3
E: What are you doing now?
F: I'm going to meet a friend. Do you want to come?
E: Where are you going?
F: Cheers. It's a place in New Street. Do you know it?
E: No.
F: It's good.
E: OK. Great. How do you get there?
F: Bus.
E: OK. Can I go the toilet first?
F: Sure. I'll meet you outside.
E: I need some money, too.
F: Me too. There's a cash machine next to the bar.

TRACK 94

1 I'm going to meet my brother tonight.
2 We're going to the park this afternoon.
3 We're going to the beach on Sunday.
4 I'm going to have a coffee now.
5 We're going to have a party tomorrow night.
6 I'm going to the pool with some friends tomorrow morning.

TRACK 96

1 I'll meet you at the hotel.
2 I'll meet you at the station.
3 I'll meet you at the bus stop at six.
4 I'll meet you there in ten minutes.
5 I'll meet you here at five o'clock.

TRACKS 97 & 98

1 I'm going to meet a friend.
2 We need to get off at the next stop.
3 When's the next train?
4 Where are you going?
5 What time are you going?
6 We need to change at Red Square.
7 I'll meet you at six.
8 How do you get there?

UNIT 6

TRACK 101

1 I have a problem at work. I need to work late.
2 I can't sleep. There's a lot of noise outside my room.
3 The weather's very bad. There's a lot of rain.
4 The flight is two hours late. We need to wait in the airport.
5 We need help, but there's no-one here.
6 There are a lot of people here. There's nowhere to sit.
7 I'm going to bed early. I'm very tired.
8 We're going the wrong way. This isn't the right train!

TRACK 102

D = Dana, B = Bryan
D: Bryan. Great to see you!
B: Hi, Dana. How are you?
D: Great.
B: Sorry I'm late! There was a problem in London.
D: Don't worry. It was on the airport website.
B: Oh, good.
D: How was the flight?
B: Not very good. The weather was bad.
D: Oh, I'm sorry. Are you tired?
B: Yeah. Where are we going now?
D: To the hotel and then we can have something to eat.
B: Oh, sorry. I had dinner on the plane. I'm not hungry.
D: That's OK. Do you want to stay in the hotel?
B: Is that OK? I did a lot yesterday and I went to bed late.
D: Of course! We can go out tomorrow.
B: Great. Thanks.

TRACK 104

1 Sorry I didn't come to class on Monday.
2 Sorry. I don't have any money.
3 Sorry. I'm very early!
4 Sorry the room isn't very big.
5 Sorry. I don't know the answer.

▶ TRACK 105

A: Hi. How are you?
B: I'm good, thanks. And you?
A: I'm OK. Sorry, I'm late.
B: Don't worry.
A: How was your journey?
B: There was a lot of traffic.
A: I know.
B: How was your day?
A: Not very good. I had a lot of problems.
B: Sorry to hear that.

▶ TRACK 106

1 Good evening. Do you have any rooms for tonight?
2 Hi. We have a booking. My name's Kim Jae-Sung.
3 Can I have your passport, please?
4 Can you write your name and address here? And sign here?
5 Do you need help with your bags?
6 Here's your key. Your room number is 351.
7 What time do we need to check out?
8 I'm sorry there's no lift. The stairs are over there.
9 What time is breakfast in the morning?
10 What's the password for the WiFi?

▶ TRACK 107

A: Hi.
B: Hello, sir. How can I help you?
A: We have a booking. My name's Kim Jae-Sung.
B: OK. Yes. Welcome. Can I have your passport, please?
A: Sure.
B: Do you have a car?
A: No.
B: OK. Can you write your name and address here? And sign here?
A: OK.
B: Here's your key. Your room number is 351. It's on the third floor.
A: Thanks.
B: Do you need help with your bags?
A: Sorry. Can you say that again?
B: Do you need help with your bags?
A: Oh. No. That's OK.
B: The lift is over there.
A: OK. What time is breakfast in the morning?
B: Seven to ten, in the restaurant. It's fifteen dollars.
A: Oh, I didn't pay?
B: No. Sorry. Your booking is not with breakfast.
A: OK. Don't worry.

▶ TRACKS 109 & 110

L = Lucy, D = Dom

Parts 1 and 2

L: Do you need somewhere to sit?
D: Yes. Can I sit here?
L: Of course. Your name's Dom, right? We met yesterday.
D: Yeah, yeah. And you're … er … Lucy.
L: That's right. Well, good morning.
D: Yes. Hi. … How was your breakfast?
L: It was good.
D: What did you have?
L: Just eggs and fruit juice. I wasn't very hungry.
D: OK.
L: And how are you? Did you sleep well?
D: Yes, thanks. You?
L: Fine, but I went to bed late.
D: What time?
L: About three in the morning.
D: Oh. What did you do?
L: I went out with some other people from here.
D: Where did you go?
L: We walked round the Old Town.
D: How was it?
L: Great. They had music in the street. We danced a lot.
D: Great. Was it busy?
L: Yeah. There were lots of people. And you? What did you do last night?
D: Not much. I stayed here.
L: OK.
D: I had dinner and I talked to some people.
L: Yeah, it's great here – people are very nice.
D: Yeah – but I didn't feel very well, so I went to bed early.
L: Oh, I'm sorry. Are you OK now?
D: Yeah, I feel fine.
L: Good.
D: Maybe I was just tired.

▶ TRACKS 111 & 112

Part 3

L: Yeah. So, what are you doing today?
D: I'm going to visit the modern art museum.
L: Oh really? Me too.
D: Oh OK. Well, do you want to go together?
L: Yeah – if that's OK.
D: Of course.
L: When are you going?
D: I'm going to have a shower first. After that?
L: Yes. Fine.
D: OK. Well, I'll meet you here. In … thirty minutes?
L: OK. What time is it now?
D: Er, 9.25.
L: Great! See you at about ten.

▶ TRACK 114

1 A: I went shopping.
  B: What did you buy?
2 A: I went to work.
  B: Where do you work?
3 A: I went out.
  B: Where did you go?
4 A: I went to my classes at the university.
  B: What do you study?
5 A: I went to the beach.
  B: Did you stay there all day?
6 A: I stayed at home.
  B: What did you do?
7 A: I watched TV.
  B: What did you see?
8 A: I went to the gym.
  B: Do you go every day?

▶ TRACK 115
1. How was your journey?
2. I had a very busy day.
3. We stayed in a hostel.
4. We had a great view of the lake.
5. What's the password for the WiFi?
6. What did you do last night?
7. I met some friends.
8. I went to the gym.

▶ TRACK 116
1. Did you go to the museum yesterday?
2. I'm going to meet some friends this afternoon.
3. There are some good places to eat in Kalamaki.
4. What time did you go to bed last night?
5. We had good weather on Saturday. We went to the beach.

GRAMMAR REFERENCE

▶ TRACK 188
1. I'm Juan. Nice to meet you.
2. This is my teacher, Lena.
3. She's my sister.
4. We're in the same class.
5. He's nice.
6. Who are they?
7. What's your name?
8. My son is three today.

▶ TRACK 189
1. His name is Karim.
2. Karen's husband is a teacher.
3. My name's Ulla.
4. Our address is 15 New Road.
5. Where's their new flat?
6. When's his party?
7. What's your cat's name?
8. Is Liam's new baby a boy or a girl?
9. What's your name?
10. What's Tomas and Pepa's phone number?

▶ TRACKS 190 & 191
1. Who's he?
2. Where is it?
3. Where are you from?
4. How much is it?
5. What day is it?
6. What's your name?
7. How old is she?
8. What time is it?
9. How much are they?
10. How are you?
11. How old are you?
12. Where is he?
13. Who's she?
14. How long is it?

▶ TRACK 192
A: Where do you live?
B: In Beppu. Do you know it?
A: No. Where is it?
B: It's a small city in the south of Japan.
A: Do you like it?
B: Yes. It's a nice place. Where do you live?
A: Birmingham. Do you know it?
B: Yes. My friend lives there!
A: What's his name?
B: Brian.
A: Do you know his family name?
B: No. Sorry. Do you like Birmingham?
A: Yes, it's OK.

▶ TRACK 194
1. do you
2. are you
3. do you
4. do you
5. are you
6. do you
7. Where do you work?
8. Where are you from?
9. When do you work?
10. Are you from here?
11. Do you know him?
12. How are you?

▶ TRACK 195
1. Where are you from?
2. Do you live here?
3. Are you OK?
4. What do you do?
5. Do you know it?

▶ TRACK 197
1. Where does he work?
2. What time does your class start?
3. Do you have a car?
4. Is it near here?
5. What does she do?
6. Does she know your mum?
7. Does he like it?
8. What does she know?

▶ TRACK 198
1. It's good.
2. It's not very hot.
3. I'm not married.
4. He's not Michel.
5. We're from Rome.
6. She's not from here.
7. This isn't very good.
8. They're very nice people.
9. That's right.
10. My sister's small.
11. My coffee's cold.
12. They aren't very big.

▶ TRACK 199
1. I'm never late.
2. We always go to church on Sunday.
3. I'm not usually busy on Thursday.
4. I normally walk to work.
5. I sometimes take the bus.
6. My wife often works in the evening.
7. My husband usually has lunch at home.
8. My brother sometimes takes my things.

TRACK 201

1. Sorry, I can't.
2. You can.
3. Can you?
4. I can't see.
5. Can I use your phone?
6. You can sit here.
7. You can't come in.
8. I can play it again.
9. Can't we leave now?
10. He can use my tablet.
11. They can't help you.
12. Can you turn off the light?

TRACK 202

1. Do you want to go for a walk?
2. I'm going swimming later.
3. I'm going for a coffee. Do you want to come?
4. We're going shopping on Saturday.
5. Do you want to go out for dinner tonight?
6. I need to go for a run.

TRACK 203

1. A: I'm going to Qatar next week.
   B: Why are you going?
   A: My company has an office there.
2. A: Do you want to go to the dinner together?
   B: Sure. What time?
   A: Eight?
3. A: We're going to Costa Rica on holiday.
   B: How long are going for?
   A: Two weeks.
4. A: I'm sorry. I'm not free tomorrow.
   B: What are you doing?
   A: I'm going to the dentist in the morning and I'm going to meet a friend at the airport in the afternoon.
5. A: I'm going to see *An American in Paris* tonight.
   B: Nice! Who are you going with?
   A: My boyfriend.
6. A: I'm going away for the weekend.
   B: Where are you going?
   A: Krakow – it's a city in Poland.

TRACK 205

1. there are some
2. there aren't any
3. there isn't a
4. there aren't any
5. Is there a
6. Are there any good places to visit?
7. There aren't any shops near here.
8. There's some parking here.
9. Are there any buses to the airport?
10. There are two cash machines there.
11. There's a shop at the end of the road.
12. There are some things in the back of the car.

TRACK 209

1. do you
2. did you
3. did you
4. do you
5. Did you know anyone there?
6. Do you want a coffee?
7. What do you do?
8. What time did you go to bed?
9. Did you live there?
10. Do you have any money?
11. Where did you go?
12. Did you sleep well?

WORKBOOK
KELLY PHILLIPS

BEGINNER
OUTCOMES

CONTENTS

01	BE	P. 96
02	LIVE, WORK, EAT	P. 102
03	LOVE, WANT, NEED	P. 108
04	WHERE AND WHEN?	P. 114
05	GOING PLACES	P. 120
06	AWAY FROM HOME	P. 126
	Audioscript	P. 132
	Answer Key	P. 136

NATIONAL GEOGRAPHIC LEARNING

ngl.cengage.com/outcomes
PASSWORD outcomes!C4#

01 BE

VOCABULARY Numbers 1–12

1 Find the numbers 1–12 in the wordsquare. Look → and ↓.

G	J	T	F	I	V	E	U	J	G
G	S	W	E	E	T	J	S	X	I
A	B	E	J	Y	H	E	E	S	S
G	F	L	Q	K	R	K	L	T	I
O	V	V	K	S	E	V	E	N	X
D	F	E	H	O	E	F	V	W	T
G	T	W	O	O	N	E	E	I	E
T	C	Z	N	B	N	I	N	E	N
J	F	O	U	R	E	I	G	H	T
A	E	Y	X	K	R	H	G	C	Z

2 🎧 1.1 Listen and circle the numbers you hear.

1 2 ③ 4 5 6 7 8 9 10 11 12

> **Learner tip**
> Start a vocabulary notebook. Write all the new words that you learn in your notebook.

LISTENING

3 🎧 1.2 Listen to the conversation and tick (✓) the correct picture (1 or 2).

4 🎧 1.2 Listen again and number the sentences in the correct order.

Ines, this is my friend Ethan.	[ ]
Hi. I'm Ines.	[ ]
Hi. Nice to meet you.	[ ]
Khalid.	[ ]
Nice to meet you.	[ ]
What's your name?	[1]
Yes. You, too, Ines.	[ ]
Yes. You, too.	[ ]

DEVELOPING CONVERSATIONS
Checking names

5 Read the conversations. Circle the correct words.
1 A: Who's (he) / she?   B: He's Greg.
2 A: Who's she?   B: He's / She's Lara.
3 A: Who are he / they?   B: Leo and Sue.
4 A: Who's he?   B: I / He don't know.

6 Complete the conversations with the words and phrases in the box.

are they	I	know	's he	's she	Who

1 A: Who's he?
   B: *I* don't know.
2 A: Who............................. ?
   B: She's Emma.
3 A: Who............................. ?
   B: He's Ben.
4 A: Who .... ?
   B: Tina and Jack.
5 A: Who's he?
   B: I don't ....
6 A: .... are they?
   B: Hugh and Poppy.

01

VOCABULARY People

7 Look at the photos. Put the letters in the correct order and write the words.

1 cdorot *doctor*
2 reetcha ....
3 ndfrie ....
4 nso ....
5 therom ....
6 ifwe ....

8 Complete the words for people with the vowels (*a, e, i, o, u*).
1 f *a* th *e* r
2 d __ __ ght __ r
3 br __ th __ r
4 h __ sb __ nd
5 s __ st __ r

9 🔊 1.3 Listen. Complete the sentences. Use words from Exercises 7 and 8.
1 Shirley: Liam is my *husband*. He's a doctor.
2 Liam: Shirley is my wife. She's a .... in an English school. This is my son, Hugh. He's nine. And she is my ...., Rebeca. She's nine, too!
3 Rebeca: Hugh's my .... He is my best ...., too. We're in the same class at school!
4 Hugh: Rebeca is my sister. My .... is a teacher and my .... is a doctor.

GRAMMAR 'm, 's, 're

10 Complete the sentences with *'m, 's, 're* or *is*.
1 He *'s* my husband.
2 Hi, I .... Oliver.
3 My name .... Sophia.
4 She .... a teacher.
5 They .... nice!
6 This .... my brother, Lucas.
7 We .... your friends.
8 You .... my doctor, right?

11 Look at the pictures and complete the sentences. Use the words from the box.

| He's | I'm | She's | They're | ~~We're~~ |

1 *We're* Poppy and Maria.
2 .... James.
3 .... Katia.
4 .... Andrew.
5 .... Zoe and Stella.

01 BE 97

01

VOCABULARY Numbers 13–22

1 🔊 1.4 Listen and circle the numbers you hear.

18	15	21	4	17	22	13	16
14	3	10	12	19	8	20	9

2 🔊 1.4 Listen and repeat.

> **Language note**
>
> Use a hyphen (-) when you write numbers after 20, for example, twenty-one and twenty-two.

3 Find the numbers 13–22 in the wordsnake.

VOCABULARY Question words

4 Circle the correct question words.
1 Who / *What time* is the English class?
2 How old / How long is your son?
3 How much / Who is lunch?
4 Who / What time is she?
5 How old / Where are you from?
6 Who / How long is the class?

5 Complete the conversations with question words.
1 A: *Where* is Paola from?
   B: She's from Brazil.
2 A: .... is the party?
   B: 9 o'clock.
3 A: .... is the coffee break?
   B: Fifteen minutes.
4 A: .... is this pen?
   B: Two euros.
5 A: .... are you?
   B: I'm twenty-two.
6 A: .... is he?
   B: He's my doctor.

GRAMMAR Questions with be

6 Read the questions. Circle the correct words.
1 Where *are* / is Elena and Niko from?
2 How old is / are Jack?
3 How long are / is the break?
4 What time are / is the class?
5 Are / Is they nice?
6 Who are / is they?
7 How much are / is coffee?
8 Is / Are you OK?

7 Write questions with these words.
1 what time / the break — *What time is the break?*
2 how much / the books
3 how / you
4 the coffee / nice
5 who / he
6 where / Akemi from
7 how old / Ava
8 how long / the classes

8 Match the answers (a–h) with the questions (1–8) in Exercise 7.
a One hour.
b Yes, it's good!
c He's my son.
d Japan.
e 11 o'clock.   *1*
f Nine pounds.
g I'm OK, thanks.
h She's 19.

GRAMMAR his, her, our, their

9 Match (1–4) with (a–d).
1 Helen's doctor   a their doctor
2 Tom's doctor   b his doctor
3 Elena and George's doctor   c her doctor
4 Noah's and my doctor   d our doctor

10 Complete the text with the words in the box.

| her | his | our | their |

> Hi! I'm Lucy and this is my husband, Dan. This is
> ¹............... flat. This is Frank and this is ²...............
> wife, Regan. Frank and Regan are English and
> ³............... flat is in Oxford. This is Maria and this is
> ⁴............... mother, Lily.

98 OUTCOMES

11 The words in bold are wrong. Write the correct words.
1 This is my sister, Nancy. This is **his** mother.   *her*
2 This is Gina and **Ethan** teacher.   ....
3 This is Harry and this is Pamela. This is **our** flat.   ....
4 This is **Sharons** father.   ....
5 I'm Ken and this is my sister. This is **their** doctor.   ....

READING

12 Look at the photos and read the invitations. Match the photos (1–3) with the parties (a–c).

a

ARIA AND TINA HAVE A NEW FLAT
Come to their party
at Flat 12, Floor 5, 19 Elm Street
This Friday (14th) 4pm – 7pm
Their phone number is 131 845 2667.

b

JOE HAS A NEW BABY BROTHER!
Come to our party!
Flat 21, Floor 2, 13 Oak Street
Friday 19th, 1pm – 4pm   Lunch at 3pm!
Mobile: 08792 627 4790
Morgan, Sian and Joe

c

I'm 21!
Come to my party at:
Sam's Restaurant, 18 Brown Street
Saturday 18th 8pm – 11pm
Camila
My phone number is 131 767 7529.

13 Read about the parties again. Are these sentences true or false? Circle T or F.
1 Aria and Tina have a new flat.   (T)   F
2 Aria and Tina's party is on Sunday.   T   F
3 Tina and Joe have a new baby.   T   F
4 Morgan's number is 08792 627 4790.   T   F
5 Camila's party is at her flat.   T   F
6 Camila's party is on Saturday.   T   F

14 Circle the correct words. Then answer the questions.
1 Who / *How long* is Aria and Tina's party?
   Three hours.
2 What / Where time is Aria and Tina's party?
   ....
3 How / What day is Morgan and Sian's party?
   ....
4 Who / How is Joe?
   ....
5 How / Where old is Camila?
   ....
6 Who / Where's Camila's party?
   ....

01

VOCABULARY Times and prices

1 Complete the words for numbers with the vowels (*a, e, i, o, u*).

e i ghty f__fty-s__v__n n__n__ty-s__x f__rty
s__v__nty s__xty-thr__ __ th__rty-tw__ tw__nty

2 Read the sentences. Are they times (T) or prices (P)? Circle T or P.
1 Our break is at ten thirty. (T) P
2 A coffee is €2.99. T P
3 Cake is three pounds fifty. T P
4 It's 2pm. T P
5 My English class is at three o'clock. T P
6 Lunch is $9.99. T P

Learner tip
A *currency* is a kind of money. Write these words for currencies in your vocabulary notebook:
$ = dollar   £ = pound   € = euro

PRONUNCIATION Numbers

3 🔊 1.5 Listen and tick (✓) the number you hear, *a* or *b*.
1 a 13 [ ] b 30 [✓]
2 a 8 [ ] b 18 [ ]
3 a $19.99 [ ] b $90.99 [ ]
4 a 14 [ ] b 40 [ ]
5 a €17.50 [ ] b €7.50 [ ]

4 🔊 1.5 Listen and repeat.

VOCABULARY In a coffee shop

5 Circle the word that is different in each group.
1 americano cappuccino (sandwich)
2 cake espresso latte
3 medium tea large
4 orange juice water small
5 sandwich large cake

DEVELOPING CONVERSATIONS
Ordering and serving drinks

6 Complete the conversation with the words in the box.

| anything | else | like | much | thanks | ~~would~~ |

A: What ¹ *would* you ² .... ?
B: How ³ .... is a small orange juice?
A: Three ninety-nine.
B: OK. A small orange juice, please.
A: Orange juice. Anything ⁴ .... ?
B: Yes – a coffee cake, please.
A: OK. ⁵ .... else?
B: No, ⁶ ....
A: That's seven ninety-nine.

7 🔊 1.6 Listen and check.

GRAMMAR not

8 Write *not* in the correct place.
                    not
1 My sandwich – it's ⌄ right.

2 It's a chocolate cake.

3 It's small – medium.

4 My cappuccino – it's hot.

5 A latte is £3.69 – £5.69!

9 Write the words in the correct order to make sentences.
1 not / It's / right
   It's not right.
2 small / not / It's
   ....
3 a coffee cake / not / It's
   ....
4 pounds / It's / five / not
   ....
5 not / is / hot / My americano
   ....

LISTENING

10 🔊 1.7 Listen to the conversation. Where are the people? Tick (✓) the correct answer.
a at a party [ ]
b at a coffee shop [ ]
c at a class [ ]

100 OUTCOMES

11 🔊 **1.7 Listen again and circle the correct words.**
A: ¹ Thanks / (Hi), what would you like, sir?
B: How much is a large ² *cake / latte*?
A: ³ *Four fifty / Four fifteen.*
B: OK. A large latte, please.
A: Anything else?
B: Yes – a chocolate cake, please.
A: Thank you! ... Here you are. Is everything OK?
B: No. My latte – it's not right.
A: What's the problem, sir?
B: This is a ⁴ *large / small* latte – not a ⁵ *large / medium.*
A: Oh, yes. Sorry. OK. That's ⁶ *nine nineteen / nine ninety.*

12 Tick (✓) what the man ordered.
1 a small latte [ ]   3 a coffee cake [ ]
2 a chocolate cake [ ]   4 a large latte [ ]

DEVELOPING WRITING Describing people

13 Circle the CAPITAL letters in the sentences.
1 (C)ome to our party at 3 (H)igh (S)treet.
2 This is my daughter, Poppy.
3 Hi, I'm Lara.
4 He's from São Paulo in Brazil.
5 This is our son, David.

14 When do we use capital letters? Choose ✓ or ✗.
1 names of people [✓]
2 times [ ]
3 names of streets [ ]
4 prices [ ]
5 cities [ ]
6 countries [ ]
7 the first word in a sentence [ ]
8 the word *I* [ ]

15 Tick the people in your life. Choose three people and write sentences. What are their names? How old are they?

friend(s) [ ]   father [ ]
brother(s) [ ]   mother [ ]
sister(s) [ ]   husband [ ]
daughter(s) [ ]   wife [ ]
son(s) [ ]

My friends are Ava and Juan. They are 15 and 17.
My father is Abdul. He's 52.

....
....
....
....

Vocabulary Builder Quiz 1

Download the Vocabulary Builder for Unit 1 and try the quiz below. Write your answers in your notebook. Then check them and record your score.

1 Are the words for food (F) or drinks (D)? Circle F or D.
1 tea   F   D
2 sandwich   F   D
3 cake   F   D
4 milk   F   D
5 chocolate   F   D
6 water   F   D
7 coffee   F   D

2 Write the words in the box in the correct place.

brother	daughter	invitation	school
Sunday	wife		

1 husband   ....
2 son   ....
3 party   ....
4 sister   ....
5 Saturday ....
6 teacher   ....

3 Circle the correct words.
1 That's a big *flat / Friday.*
2 Yes, that's *same / right.*
3 I don't *like / know.*
4 What's your *name / doctor*?
5 Nice to *meet / come* you!
6 A fresh orange *cappuccino / juice*, please.

4 Complete the words in the sentences with the vowels (*a, e, i, o, u*).
1 Where are you fr__m?
2 Gina is in my English cl__ss.
3 Stavros is my best fr__ __nd.
4 How long is the br__ __k?
5 __nyth__ng else?
6 How much is a m__d__ __m espresso?

Score ___/25

Wait a couple of weeks and try the quiz again. Compare your scores.

02 LIVE, WORK, EAT

VOCABULARY My home

1 Find nine words related to people's homes in the wordsnake.

road dw south ky park mn village as
hn centre cd k city
pl flats qw house br north hol

2 Look at the pictures and numbers 1–8. Write words from Exercise 1 next to the correct number.

1 village
2 ....
3 ....
4 ....
5 ....
6 ....
7 ....
8 ....

1 village

GRAMMAR Present simple

3 Choose the correct words.
1 They *walk* / *walks* on the road to the centre.
2 It *take* / *takes* twenty minutes.
3 I *lives* / *live* in a village.
4 She *has* / *have* a small house.
5 You *has* / *have* a big flat.
6 We *like* / *likes* the centre.
7 He's from Ottawa. He *know* / *knows* the city.

> **Language note**
>
> I / you / we / they **have**, but he / she / it **has**.

4 Complete the sentences with the present simple form of the verbs in brackets.
1 My brother *knows* Peter. They're friends. (know)
2 My mother and father .... in a small village. (live)
3 We .... you. You're in our class! (know)
4 I .... their flat. It's big. (like)
5 You .... two parks in your city. (have)
6 We walk to school. It .... five minutes. (take)
7 My friend Maria .... in Chile. (live)

5 Complete the text with the words in the box.

| has | have | knows | ~~like~~ | likes | lives |

My name is Stella and this is my city, Athens. I ¹ *like* my city. Athens ² .... houses, flats, roads – and nice parks! I ³ .... a brother. His name's Spyros. He ⁴ .... in a small village called Kastania with his wife, Sophia. He ⁵ .... his village – it's great! He ⁶ .... the people in the village.

102 OUTCOMES

GRAMMAR
Present simple questions: *do you*

6 Choose the correct words.
1 *Do you like / You like* your village?
2 *Who you live / Who do you live* with?
3 *You do have / Do you have* a flat or a house?
4 *Where is / Where do* you live?
5 *Do you know / Do you knows* my father?
6 *Do you walk / You walk* here?

7 Match the answers (a–f) with the questions (1–6) in Exercise 6.
a A flat. [ ]
b My wife and baby son. [ ]
c Yes. He's my doctor. [ ]
d On Hill Road. [ ]
e Yes. It takes ten minutes. [ ]
f Yes. It's nice and has a big park. [*1*]

8 Read the conversations. Write questions using the words. Use a question word in questions 4–6.
1 A: you / live with your mother and father
 Do you live with your mother and father?
 B: Yes. And my sister.
2 A: you / like my husband's village
 ....?
 B: Yes. It's nice.
3 A: you / have a big house
 ....?
 B: No. It's small.
4 A: you / live
 ....?
 B: I live on Elm Road.
5 A: you / know here
 ....?
 B: I know Ines and Khalid.
6 A: you / have a flat
 ....?
 B: I have a flat in Rio.

DEVELOPING CONVERSATIONS
And you?

9 Number the parts of each conversation 1–3.
1 I'm twenty. And you? [*2*]
 I'm eighteen. [*3*]
 How old are you? [*1*]
2 I'm great. [ ]
 Fine, thanks. And you? [ ]
 How are you? [ ]
3 Caleb. And you? [ ]
 Marianna. [ ]
 What's your name? [ ]

10 Complete the conversations with the answers in the box.

| ~~I'm OK.~~ | Near the park. | No, it's very big. |
| Suki. | Yes, a sister. | |

1 A: How are you? B: Fine, thanks. And you?
 A: *I'm OK.*
2 A: What's your name? B: Cristiano. And you?
 A: ....
3 A: Where do you live? B: On Grant Road. And you?
 A: ....
4 A: Do you have a brother or sister?
 B: A brother. And you?
 A: ....
5 A: Do you like London? B: Yes, it's great. And you?
 A ....

LISTENING

11 🔊 2.1 Listen to the conversation. Tick (✓) the things the people talk about.
1 names [✓]
2 times [ ]
3 prices [ ]
4 homes [ ]
5 brothers and sisters [ ]
6 mothers and fathers [ ]
7 friends [ ]

12 🔊 2.1 Listen again. Circle the correct words.
Angelina:
1 lives *on Venice Road* / *in Westville*.
2 lives near *Sebastian* / *their school*.
3 *walks* / *takes a bus* to school.

Sebastian:
4 lives in *a flat* / *a house*.
5 has a *big* / *small* home.
6 lives with his *mother and father* / *friends*.

02 LIVE, WORK, EAT 103

02

VOCABULARY Jobs

1 Put the letters in the correct order. Write the jobs next to the correct photos (a–h).
1. usb ridrev
2. mmu
3. serun
4. erdtier
5. nttsued
6. eahcetr
7. tiware
8. rokw ni na iceffo

a *bus driver*
b ....
c ....
d ....
e ....
f ....
g ....
h ....

Learner tip

Learn new words every day. Have a friend test you. It's a great way to remember new words.

GRAMMAR Present simple: *don't (do not)*

2 Write the words in the correct order to make sentences.
1. in / I / a / live / flat / don't
   I don't live in a flat.
2. big / don't / cities / They / like
   ....
3. don't / to / go / school / We
   ....
4. have / don't / You / job / a
   ....
5. an / don't / in / office / They / work
   ....

3 Write three sentences that are true for you. Use *don't*.
....
....
....

GRAMMAR Plural / no plural

4 Are the words correct? Write (✓) or (✗).
1. doctors [✓]
2. jobs [ ]
3. childs [ ]
4. moneys [ ]
5. hours [ ]
6. waters [ ]
7. persons [ ]
8. teachers [ ]
9. waiters [ ]

Language note

Most nouns form their plural with *s*.
road – road**s**   mother – mother**s**
Some plurals are irregular.
child – child**ren** (childs)   person – **people** (peoples)

5 Write the plurals of the words. Write (✗) for words with no plural.
1. nurse — *nurses*
2. child — ....
3. student — ....
4. money — ....
5. person — ....
6. flat — ....
7. work — ....
8. drink — ....
9. mum — ....
10. area — ....

6 The words in bold are wrong. Write the correct words.
1. I am a bus driver. The money **are** good.   *is*
2. We don't have a lot of **times**.   ....
3. This is my school. The people **is** nice.   ....
4. The **house** are small.   ....
5. Some nurses **is** great.   ....
6. James has two **flat**.   ....

104 OUTCOMES

READING

7 Read the four texts. Where do the people live? Write the country.
1 Loretta ....
2 Juan ....
3 Channary ....
4 Hans ....

8 Are the sentences true or false? Circle T or F.
1 Loretta's job is in the north of Toronto. T (F)
2 Loretta works with nice people. T F
3 Juan works in a small school. T F
4 Juan likes his students. T F
5 Channary works in an office. T F
6 Channary lives in a big city. T F
7 Hans lives with three people. T F
8 Hans has a lot of free time. T F

WORK IN A DIFFERENT COUNTRY!

December 13
STAR RATING ★★★★
Hi, I'm Loretta. I'm from New Zealand, but now I live and work in Toronto, Canada. I live in an area called Scarborough. I work in an office in the south of the city. It takes 20 minutes by bus. The job's OK. I like the people I work with, but the money is bad.

December 21
STAR RATING ★★★★★
Hello. My name's Channary. I'm from Cambodia. Now I live and work in Sweden. I work for a bus company. I'm a bus driver. I like my job. Traffic isn't bad in Avesta – it's a small city. The money is good and I don't work a lot of hours – 15 a week. I have lots of time with my friends and my two dogs!

December 19
STAR RATING ★★★
Hello. I'm Juan. I'm from Spain, but I'm a teacher in Leeds, England. My job's OK, but I don't like the school. It's big and it's in the centre. It's 50 minutes by train from my flat. The students are great, but I don't like some classes.

December 30
STAR RATING ★★★★
My name's Hans. I'm from Germany, but now I live and work in Poland – in an area in the north of Warsaw. I live in a house with three people from different countries. I'm a waiter. It's OK. I like the other waiters, but I don't like the hours. I go to work from 4 to 9. And I have classes too, from 8 to 3. That's a lot of hours!

DEVELOPING WRITING
Writing a description of yourself

Acacia's blog
Profile
1 [a] Acacia Gonzales
2 [   ] 19
3 [   ] **From:** Mexico
4 [   ] **Live in:** Comitán (city); Chiapas (area); in the south of Mexico
5 [   ] **Home:** flat
6 [   ] **Live with:** my mother and father
7 [   ] Student at Instituto Tecnológico

9 Read Acacia's profile on her blog. Match the information (1–7) to the questions (a–g).
a What's your name?
b Where do you live?
c How old are you?
d Where are you from?
e Do you live in a house or a flat?
f What do you do?
g Who do you live with?

10 Complete the blog with information about Acacia.

Hi, I'm [1] *Acacia Gonzales*. I'm [2] .... I'm from [3] ....

I live in a city called [4] ....
It's in an area called [5] ...., in the [6] .... of Mexico.

I live in a small flat with [7] ....
It's on a big road, near a small park. I don't work. I go to a university called [8] ....

11 Answer the questions in Exercise 9 about yourself. Write a blog profile for you.

02

VOCABULARY Food and drinks

1 Circle the word that is different in each group.
1 burger   chicken   (orange juice)
2 salad   ice cream   cake
3 meat   fish   drinks
4 vegetables   salad   coffee cake
5 water   meat   fruit juice

2 Look at the pictures and complete the crossword.

1 J	U	I	2 C	E

(crossword with 1 across: JUICE; 3 across; 5 across; 2 down; 3 down; 4 down)

Across →
1   3   5

Down ↓
2   3   4

GRAMMAR like / don't like

3 Complete the sentences with like ☺, don't like ☹ or love ♥.
1 I *don't like* meat. ☹
2 Burgers and chips! I .... them! ♥
3 I .... tea and coffee. ☺
4 Fish? No, thanks. I .... it. ☹
5 I .... ice cream! ☺
6 I .... fresh fruit and salads. ♥

4 Complete the sentences with like, don't like or love so they are true for you.
1 I .... fruit.
2 I .... fish and seafood.
3 I .... vegetarian dishes.
4 I .... carrot cake.
5 I .... cheese pizza.
6 I .... bacon sandwiches.

5 Complete the conversations with it or them.
1 A: I love ice cream.
   B: Me, too. I love *it*!
2 A: I love burgers.
   B: Me, too. I love .... with chips.
3 A: I don't like strawberries.
   B: I don't like ...., but I like oranges.
4 A: I don't like bacon.
   B: Oh? I love ....
5 A: I like fruit juice.
   B: Yes, I like ...., too.
6 A: I like kebabs.
   B: No! I don't like ....!

DEVELOPING CONVERSATIONS
Ordering food

6 Write the words in the correct order to make sentences from a conversation in a restaurant. Who says the sentence, the waiter (W) or a customer (C)?
1 with / else / your fish? / Anything
   Anything else with your fish?   [W]
2 order? / Are you / to / ready   [   ]
   ....
3 please. / Chips,   [   ]
   ....
4 please. / fish, / The   [   ]
   ....
5 much / a salad? / is / How   [   ]
   ....
6 you? / And   [   ]
   ....
7 pounds. / ten / It's   [   ]
   ....
8 thanks. / Oh! / No,   [   ]
   ....
9 rice / or chips? / With   [   ]
   ....
10 with chips / A burger / for me / Yes.   [   ]
   ....

7 Put the sentences from Exercise 6 in the correct order. Write the conversation.
W: *Are you ready to order?*
C: ....
W: ....
C: ....
W: ....
C: ....
W: ....
C: ....
W: ....
C: ....

8 ⚫ 2.2 Listen and check your answers.

106 OUTCOMES

LISTENING

9 🔊 **2.3 Listen to four conversations. Match the conversations (1–4) to the pictures (a–d).**

10 🔊 **2.3 Listen again. Are the sentences true or false? Circle T or F.**

Conversation 1
1 The woman likes espresso.   T   F
2 The woman likes tea.   T   F
Conversation 2
3 The boy loves cake and ice cream. T   F
4 The boy doesn't like vegetables.   T   F
Conversation 3
5 The man wants a table for two.   T   F
6 The people don't know English.   T   F
Conversation 4
7 A coke is five euros thirteen.   T   F
8 The man says the coke is expensive. T F

PRONUNCIATION /z/ and /s/

11 Read these words and think about the sound of the letters in bold. What are the two different sounds?

| bu**s** driver | doctor**s** | doe**s** | flat**s** |
| hour**s** | hou**s**e | live**s** | **s**outh |

12 🔊 **2.4 Listen and write the words in the correct place.**

/z/	/s/
	bus driver

13 🔊 **2.4 Listen again and check your answers.**

Vocabulary Builder Quiz 2

Download the Vocabulary Builder for Unit 2 and try the quiz below. Write your answers in your notebook. Then check them and record your score.

1 Are the words for people (P) or places (PL)? Circle P or PL.
1 city   P   PL
2 village   P   PL
3 driver   P   PL
4 nurse   P   PL
5 centre   P   PL
6 waiter   P   PL
7 student   P   PL

2 Circle the word that is different in each group.
1 great   expensive   good
2 train   taxi   person
3 bacon   chicken   carrot
4 salad   ice cream   tomato
5 minute   burger   meat
6 office   dog   shop

3 Write the words in the box in the correct place.

| chips   dad   far   small   south   vegetables |

1 fruit and ....
2 north and ....
3 mum and   ....
4 big and   ....
5 near and   ....
6 fish and   ....

4 Complete the words in the sentences with the vowels (a, e, i, o, u).
1 I l__v__ with two friends.
2 I don't like my job. I work a lot of h__ __rs.
3 Westville is in an __r__ __ called Pictou County.
4 Do you have a h__ __s__ or a flat?
5 I don't work. I'm r__t__r__d.
6 The __n__v__rs__ty is on Brant Road.

Score ___/25

Wait a couple of weeks and try the quiz again. Compare your scores.

02 LIVE, WORK, EAT

03 LOVE, WANT, NEED

VOCABULARY Adjectives

1 Match the adjectives (1–4) with their opposites (a–d).
1 bad   a hot
2 big   b small
3 cold   c old
4 new   d good

> **Learner tip**
> When you learn new adjectives, write them with their opposites (≠).

2 Complete the adjectives with the vowels (a, e, i, o, u).
1 d*ificu*lt
2 _xp_ns_v_
3 gr__t
4 h_ngry
5 m_rr__d
6 n_c_
7 t_r_d
8 w_ll

3 Look at the photos and the sentences. Circle the correct word. Then complete the sentence with *a* or *an*.

1 It's *a* cold / **hot** pizza.
2 It's .... big / married house.
3 It's .... old / new flat.
4 He's .... small / hungry man.
5 It's .... difficult / expensive coffee shop.
6 He's .... tired / new man.

Language note

Vowels are *a, e, i, o, u*. All the other letters in the alphabet are consonants.
We use *a* before words which start with a consonant.
a big city, **a n**ew flat
We use *an* before words which start with a vowel.
an old house, **an E**nglish class

PRONUNCIATION
Saying words together

4 3.1 Listen. Which two words sound like one word? Draw lines.
1 an‿expensive flat   3 an English teacher
2 an orange bus   4 an old village

5 3.1 Listen again and repeat.

GRAMMAR Negatives with *be*

6 Circle the correct words.
1 She *'m not* / *'s not* my teacher.
2 They *'re not* / *'s not* expensive flats.
3 We *'re not* / *'m not* from China.
4 I *'re not* / *'m not* tired.
5 It *'re not* / *'s not* a big hotel.

7 The words in bold are incorrect. Write the correct words.
1 It **'re not** a very good coffee shop.   *'s not*
2 We **'m not** very well.   ....
3 He **'re not** married, right?   ....
4 They **'m not** new students.   ....
5 I **'re not** your waiter.   ....

8 Complete the conversations with *'m not*, *'s not* or *'re not*.
1 A: Your room is great!
   B: Thanks. And it *'s not* expensive.
2 A: Do you know Maria and Tia?
   B: No, they .... in my class.
3 A: Do you know the city?
   B: No, we .... from here.
4 A: Is Ella his wife?
   B: No, he .... married.
5 A: Do you want a sandwich?
   B: No, thanks. I .... very hungry.

108 OUTCOMES

LISTENING

9 🔊 **3.2 Listen to four conversations. Match the pictures (a–d) with the conversations (1–4).**

a [ ] b [ ] c [ ] d [ ]

10 🔊 **3.2 Listen again. Number the questions in the correct order.**
   a How's the weather? [ ]
   b How's your son? [ ]
   c How's your job? [ ]
   d How's your flat? [ ]

11 Complete the sentences from the conversations with the words in the box.

| difficult | expensive | hot | very good | ~~very well~~ |

Conversation 1
1 A: He's not *very well*.
   B: Oh, no! I'm sorry.
Conversation 2
2 A: It's good, but flats in the city are ....
   B: Yes!
Conversation 3
3 A: It's very .... I love it.
   B: Oh. It's not normally hot in Canada.
Conversation 4
4 A: It's not .... How's your job?
   B: The same. And it's ....!

12 🔊 **3.2 Listen again and check your answers.**

DEVELOPING CONVERSATIONS
Responding to news

13 Complete the table with the sentences in the box.

~~It's very cold here.~~	My chicken's not hot.
She's very well, thanks.	His job is difficult.
It's very nice.	The other students are great.

Good news ☺	Bad news ☹
....	*It's very cold here.*
....	....
....	....
....	....

14 Complete the conversations with the sentences in Exercise 13.
   1 A: How's the weather in Moscow?
      B: I don't like it. *It's very cold here.*
   2 A: How's your brother?
      B: He's very tired. ....
         And the money's not very good.
   3 A: How's your sister?
      B: Leah? ....
   4 A: How's your food?
      B: It's very bad. ....
   5 A: How's university?
      B: I love it! ....
   6 A: How's your hotel?
      B: .... And it's new!

15 Respond to the news in Exercise 14. Write *Oh, good* or *I'm sorry* for each conversation.
   Conversation 1:   *I'm sorry.*
   Conversation 2:   ....
   Conversation 3:   ....
   Conversation 4:   ....
   Conversation 5:   ....
   Conversation 6:   ....

03

VOCABULARY go, take, want

Learner tip

We use some verbs in English a lot. When you learn verbs like *go*, *take* and *want*, try to learn some of the nouns that we use them with, too.

1 The words in bold are incorrect. Write the correct words (*goes*, *takes* or *wants*).
1 My father **goes** a shower every day.   *takes*
2 Anna **wants** shopping on Saturday.   ....
3 My brother is hungry. He **goes** a salad.   ....
4 He **takes** to the park on Friday.   ....
5 The bus **wants** a long time.   ....
6 The baby **goes** some milk.   ....
7 My sister **goes** the train to school.   ....

2 Complete the texts with *goes*, *takes* or *wants*.

My friend, Muhammed, [1] *takes* the bus every day. He [2] .... to the gym. He [3] .... a shower every day, too. He [4] .... a long time.

My sister [5] .... shopping every day. She [6] .... to buy new clothes. They are expensive! She [7] .... to the coffee shop every day, too. She [8] .... to meet her friends.

Helen loves hot weather. She [9] .... to Cuba – she [10] .... on holiday. She [11] .... photos. Her photos are great!

GRAMMAR Present simple: doesn't

3 Make the sentences negative.
1 He likes fish.
   He doesn't like fish.
2 Leo knows my teacher.
   ....
3 The train takes a long time.
   ....
4 My brother wants to go to the party.
   ....
5 The bus goes to the city.
   ....
6 She lives in a new house.
   ....

Learner tip

He / She / It goes, but *he / she / it doesn't go* (NOT *doesn't goes*).

4 Write the words in the correct order to make sentences.
1 the / doesn't / train / She / take
   She doesn't take the train.
2 hotel / He / like / doesn't / his
   ....
3 go / doesn't / shopping / every day / Maria
   ....
4 have / doesn't / My mother / car / a
   ....
5 to / long / doesn't / walk / school / to / It / take
   ....
6 doesn't / my / near / gym / The number 10 bus / go
   ....

5 Complete the conversations with the verbs.
1 A: My friend *wants* a pizza. She's hungry.   (want)
   B: My friend's not hungry.
      He .... to eat.   (not want)
2 A: My brother .... two daughters.   (have)
   B: That's nice. My brother ....
      children.   (not have)
3 A: My mother .... the bus
      to work.   (take)
   B: My mother .... the bus.   (not like)
4 A: The train .... a long time
      to get to the centre.   (take)
   B: I know. My father .... it.   (not take)

110 OUTCOMES

GRAMMAR
Present simple questions: *does*

6 Match the questions (1–6) with the answers (a–f).
1 What does your brother do? [*f*]
2 Why does she want a big house? [ ]
3 How long does it take to get to the city? [ ]
4 Where does your sister work? [ ]
5 How does he come to school? [ ]
6 Does she have any children? [ ]

a In an office.
b He walks.
c She wants a lot of children!
d Twenty minutes.
e Yes, a son and a daughter.
f He's a doctor.

7 The words in bold are incorrect. Write the correct words.
1 A: **Who** does he want a new car?   *Why*
   B: His car is very old.
2 A: **What** does your brother work?   ....
   B: In a coffee shop.
3 A: **What** does she come to university?   ....
   B: She takes the bus.
4 A: **How** time does she go to work?   ....
   B: Nine o'clock.
5 A: **Where** does your sister do?   ....
   B: She's a nurse.
6 A: **How** does she go on holiday with?   ....
   B: Her husband and children.

8 Look at the answers and write the questions. Use the question words in the box and the verbs in brackets.

| ~~How long~~ | What | When | Where (x2) |

1 A: *How long does the bus take?*   (take)
   B: The bus takes fifty minutes.
2 A: ....?   (do)
   B: My brother's a bus driver.
3 A: ....?   (work)
   B: Steven works in a school.
4 A: .... to the gym?   (go)
   B: She goes to the gym on Fridays.
5 A: .... at two o'clock?   (go)
   B: He goes to the park at two o'clock.

READING

9 Read the four texts. Who likes the things in his / her life? Tick (✓) the people.

Lucia [ ]   Ahmed [ ]   Greta [ ]   Vincenzo [ ]

Language note

A year is 365 days. There are 12 *months* in a year.

It's a new year!
What do you want in your life?

LUCIA   11:05, 1 JANUARY
I work for six days a week. I'm a doctor. I have a lot of money, but I don't have a lot of free time. That's OK. Money's important to me. My life is great. I don't want anything else!

AHMED   13:20, 1 JANUARY
I'm a nurse. I live in a bad area of the city. I like houses, but I don't like flats. I want a house – a big house in a good area of the city. I want to have a family. I want a lot of children. But it's very difficult.

GRETA   13:30, 1 JANUARY
It's my birthday this month (28th), but I don't want a party – I don't like them. But I want some things. I want $50 and a new phone. I don't like my phone. It's old!

VINCENZO   14:16, 1 JANUARY
I have a great job. I only work for three days a week. My wife works in a big office in the city. I have a son and a daughter. We are all well. We go on holidays to nice places. I like all the things in my life.

10 Read the questions. Circle the correct words.
1 *Does* / When Lucia work a lot?
2 Who / What is Lucia's job?
3 Where / What time does Ahmed live?
4 Does / What Ahmed live in a house or a flat?
5 Does / When Greta like birthday parties?
6 How much / Who money does Greta want for her birthday?
7 Why / Is Vincenzo married?
8 What / Does Vincenzo have children?

11 Tick (✓) the correct answers for the questions in Exercise 10.
1 a Yes.   [✓]   b No.   [ ]
2 a She's a teacher. [ ]   b She's a doctor. [ ]
3 a In a bad area.   [ ]   b In a good area. [ ]
4 a A house.   [ ]   b A flat.   [ ]
5 a Yes.   [ ]   b No.   [ ]
6 a $28.   [ ]   b $50.   [ ]
7 a Yes.   [ ]   b No.   [ ]
8 a Yes.   [ ]   b No.   [ ]

03 LOVE, WANT, NEED   111

03

VOCABULARY Things

1 Look at the pictures and complete the crossword.

```
    1
    S
2   O   3
    A
4   P       5
        6
    7
        8
```

Across →

2   4   6

7   8

Down ↓

1   3   5

2 Circle the word that is different in each group.

1 towel   soap   (map)
2 toothbrush   pen   toothpaste
3 money   dictionary   book
4 brush   mobile   charger
5 coat   clothes   food

DEVELOPING CONVERSATIONS
Asking for help in conversation

3 Complete the conversation with the words in the box.

| again | Can | English | How | say | ~~Sorry~~ |

Emma: Where are you from, Bandile?
Bandile: Buenos Aires.
Emma: ¹ *Sorry*? Can you ² .... that again?
Bandile: Buenos Aires, in Argentina.
Emma: Great. Welcome to London! Are you tired?
Bandile: Sorry. ³ .... you say that
         ⁴ ....?
Emma: Are you tired?
Bandile: Er ... yes. I'm hot and tired. I need to take a shower.
Emma: Oh, yes. Of course. Do you want anything?
Bandile: Do you have ... er, ... for my shower ...
Emma: A towel?
Bandile: No, I have a towel. I need some ... er, *seep*.
         ⁵ .... do you say *seep* in
         ⁶ ....?
Emma: Soap!

4 🔊 3.3 Listen and check your answers.

GRAMMAR *a* and *any*

5 Write the words and phrases in the box in the correct column.

| ~~bags~~ | book | brush | coat | food |
| local money | map | mobile | other shoes | toothpaste |

Do you have a ...?	Do you have any ...?
....	*bags*
....	....
....	....
....	....
....	....

6 Choose the correct answers.

1 I don't have *a* / *any* other soap.
2 I don't need *a* / *anything* else.
3 Do you need *a* / *any* milk?
4 Do you want *a* / *anything* ?
5 I don't have *a* / *any* pen.
6 Do you have *a* / *any* flat?
7 Do you have *a* / *any* maps?
8 I don't want *a* / *any* water.
9 Do you need *a* / *any* toothpaste?
10 Do you want *a* / *any* other drinks?
11 I don't want *a* / *any* money.

7 Complete the sentences so they are true for you. Write two or three things for each sentence. Use the words in the box or your own ideas.

big	expensive	good	new	old
car	clothes	flat	food	house
job	mobile	shoes		

1 I don't have ....
2 I don't want ....
3 I don't need ....

DEVELOPING WRITING
Writing an email

8 Read the email and tick (✓) the correct answers.
1 Ismini is Sian's
   a teacher. [ ]
   b friend. [ ]
2 The email is about
   a Ismini's life. [ ]
   b Ismini's things. [ ]

Sent | Chat | Attach | Font

Hi Sian,
Thanks for your email. I like my new job – it's great. I don't like the city! My new school's not near my flat. I go by bus and it takes me an hour. At the end of the day, I'm very tired. I want to work in a school near my flat. I want to walk to work and have more free time. But it's very difficult. I need more money!
Love,
Ismini

---

9 Read the email again. Match (1–7) with (a–g).
1 Ismini likes   [b]   a an hour.
2 Ismini doesn't like   [   ]   b her new job.
3 Ismini goes   [   ]   c more free time.
4 The bus takes   [   ]   d the city.
5 Ismini wants   [   ]   e more money.
6 Ismini wants to   [   ]   f to her job by bus.
7 Ismini needs   [   ]   g work in a school near her flat.

10 Write an email to a friend about your life. Write about things you have, things you want and things you don't want. Say why. Use the email in Exercise 8 to help you.

Vocabulary Builder Quiz 3

Download the Vocabulary Builder for Unit 3 and try the quiz below. Write your answers in your notebook. Then check them and record your score.

1 Circle the correct words.
1 **read** a book / only
2 **buy** brush / clothes
3 **go** shopping / work
4 **have** a shower / weather
5 **get** by train / married
6 **go on** holiday / university

2 Write the words in the box in the correct place.

charger	paste	phone	room	time (x2)

1 hotel   ....
2 free   ....
3 mobile   ....
4 tooth   ....
5 phone   ....
6 a long   ....

3 Complete the words in the sentences with the vowels (*a, e, i, o, u*).
1 It's v__ry hot! It's 32°C!
2 I need a sandwich. I'm h__ngry.
3 English is d__ff__c__lt, but I like it.
4 Do you have any __th__r paper?
5 Do you like the l__c__l food?
6 This is an __xp__ns__v__ charger. It's $50!
7 *Bad, new* and *happy* are __dj__ct__v__s.

4 Match the beginnings (1–6) with the endings (a–f).
1 I'm cold and   a a pen.
2 I like local   b tired.
3 I need soap and   c well.
4 Her home is old and   d a towel.
5 I'm not good. I'm not   e food.
6 I want to write your   f small.
  phone number. I need

Score ___/25

Wait a couple of weeks and try the quiz again. Compare your scores.

04 WHERE AND WHEN?

VOCABULARY Places

1 Write the words in the box in the correct place.

| machine | market | park | ~~pool~~ | shop | station |

1 swimming *pool*
2 cash ....
3 train ....
4 car ....
5 super......................................
6 clothes ....

2 Complete the words with the vowels (*a, e, i, o, u*).

1 ch *u* rch
2 c __ f __
3 h __ sp __ t __ l
4 r __ st __ __ r __ nt
5 p __ rk
6 b __ nk
7 c __ n __ m __
8 h __ t __ l
9 m __ rk __ t

3 Label the photos with words from Exercises 1 and 2.

1 *church*
2 ....

GRAMMAR *Is there ... ? / There's ...*

4 Circle the correct words.
1 *Is there* / *There's* a train station near here?
2 *There's* / *Is there* a gym next to my office.
3 No, *there's* / *there isn't* a cash machine on this road, but there is a bank.
4 *Is there* / *There's* a swimming pool in the park.
5 No, *there isn't* / *there's* a bank near here. There's one in town.
6 *Is there* / *There's* a church in your village?
7 *There isn't* / *There's* a good clothes shop on this road, but it's expensive.
8 *There isn't* / *Is there* a market in this town?

5 Complete the conversation with *Is there*, *there's* and *there isn't*.

A: ¹ *Is there* a restaurant near here?
B: No, ² ....
A: OK. ³ .... a café? I'm very hungry!
B: No, sorry, ⁴ .... one on this road.
A: Oh. ⁵ .... a supermarket?
B: Yes, ⁶ .... one next to the cinema! They have sandwiches.

6 🔊 4.1 Listen and check your answers.

3 ....
4 ....
5 ....
6 ....
7 ....
8 ....
9 ....
10 ....

114 OUTCOMES

Vocabulary Extra
Prepositions and directions

7 Circle the correct words to label the pictures.

1 *on* / in
2 on / next to
3 on the left / in
4 at the end / near
5 near / on
6 in / on the corner
7 at / down the road
8 on the right / on the left

8 Complete the sentences with the words in the box.

| at | ~~down~~ | in | near | next | on (x2) | right |

1 Take the first road *down* here on the left.
2 The cash machine is .... to the café.
3 The café is .... here – it isn't far.
4 The car park is .... this road.
5 The hotel has a swimming pool – it's .... the hotel.
6 My house is .... the end of this road.
7 The supermarket is .... the corner.
8 The bank is down this road, on the ....

Developing conversations *called*

9 🔊 4.2 Complete the sentences with the words in the box. Then listen and check.

| café | cinema | clothes shop | restaurant | ~~town~~ |

1 A: Do you know a *town* called Southsea?
   B: No, is it far?
2 On Park Road, there's a .... called Nice and New. I often go shopping there.
3 There's a nice .... called Angelo's near my house. It has great pizza!
4 A: There's a .... called the Odeon there.
   B: Yes, do you want to see a film?
5 A: Do you know a .... called The CoffeeShop?
   B: Yes, it's very expensive.

Listening

10 🔊 4.3 Listen to three conversations about places. Match the pictures (a–c) with the conversations (1–3).

11 🔊 4.3 Match the sentence beginnings (1–6) to their endings (a–f). Then listen and check.

1 Do you know a café   *e*
2 There are some cafés near here,
3 No, there isn't a cash machine,
4 The bank is on
5 It's near a hospital
6 St Ann's is on the corner, on the right,

a and the swimming pool is on the left.
b but there's a bank on Maple Road.
c called St Ann's.
d but I don't know their names.
e called the Big Cappuccino on this road?
f the right.

04 WHERE AND WHEN 115

04

PRONUNCIATION Syllable stress

Language note

A *syllable* is a part of a word that has a vowel sound (*a, e, i, o, u*).
The word *park* has one syllable.
The word *café* has two syllables: ca-fé.
The word *cinema* has three syllables: ci-ne-ma.

1 **4.4 Listen to these words and tick (✓) the number of syllables in each word.**
   1 bank   1 syllable [✓]   2 syllables [ ]
   2 station   1 syllable [ ]   2 syllables [ ]
   3 hospital   2 syllables [ ] 3 syllables [ ]
   4 market   1 syllable [ ]   2 syllables [ ]
   5 supermarket 3 syllables [ ] 4 syllables [ ]
   6 church   1 syllable [ ]   2 syllables [ ]

Language note

We often stress one syllable in a word, e.g. **doc**tor, **tea**cher, **fa**ther

2 **4.5 Listen to four words. Underline the stressed syllable.**
   1 station
   2 hospital
   3 market
   4 supermarket

VOCABULARY Days and times of day

3 **Write the days of the week in the correct order.**

| Friday | Monday | Saturday | ~~Sunday~~ | Thursday |
| Tuesday | Wednesday | | | |

   1 Sunday
   2 ....
   3 ....
   4 ....
   5 ....
   6 ....
   7 ....

4 **Circle the word that is different in each group.**
   1 today   tomorrow   (night)
   2 yesterday   afternoon   tomorrow
   3 evening   yesterday   morning
   4 morning   night   today
   5 afternoon   evening   tomorrow

5 **Complete the text with the words in the box.**

| afternoon | evening | from | morning | night | to |

I get to work in the [1]............ at 8. I have lunch at 1. Then I work [2]............ 2 in the [3]............ to 6. In the [4]............ I get to my house at 7 and I am very tired. At [5]............ I usually sleep from 11 [6]............ 6.30.

6 **Complete the groups with the correct days.**

| Friday | Monday | Saturday | ~~Thursday~~ |
| Tuesday | Wednesday | | |

   1 Today: Wednesday   Tomorrow: *Thursday*
      Yesterday: ....
   2 Today: ....   Tomorrow: Sunday
      Yesterday: ....
   3 Today: Tuesday   Tomorrow: ....
      Yesterday: ....

GRAMMAR
Adverbs of frequency

7 **Write the words in the box in the correct place.**

| always | ~~never~~ | normally | sometimes | usually |

100% ....
75% ....
....
25% ....
0% *never*

8 **Complete the sentences with adverbs of frequency.**
   1 You *always* go shopping on Saturday morning. (100%)
   2 We .... go swimming in the evening. (25%)
   3 She .... walks to her office. (0%)
   4 He .... takes the train to the city centre. (75%)
   5 They .... go to Mexico on holiday. (65%)

9 **Complete the sentences so that they are true for you.**
   1 I always .... in the morning.
   2 I usually .... in the afternoon.
   3 I sometimes .... in the evening.
   4 I never .... on Saturday.
   5 I normally .... on Sunday.

116 OUTCOMES

Reading

10 Read the article and tick (✓) the best title.
   a   The Working Week   [ ]
   b   My Weekend   [ ]
   c   Shops in Canada   [ ]

> by Janet Ferguson
>
> I'm from Nova Scotia, Canada. It's a great place.
>
> In Nova Scotia, people usually work 40 hours a week. Lots of people have Sunday free. I'm a teacher and I work in a school in a small village. I always have Saturday and Sunday free.
>
> On Saturday, I usually take the bus to the city. I sometimes go to a supermarket called Sobey's and I sometimes go to a clothes shop called Winners.
>
> On Sunday, I normally go to the market in my village. It always opens at 10 in the morning and closes at 4 in the afternoon. I always buy fresh fruit at the market. I meet friends at our favourite café in the evening.
>
> I like my job, but I love weekends!

11 Circle the correct words.
   1   People in Nova Scotia *always* / *usually* work 40 hours a week.
   2   Janet *never* / *always* has Sunday free.
   3   Janet *normally* / *sometimes* takes the bus to the city.
   4   The market in Janet's village is *always* / *never* open in the morning on Sunday.

12 Answer the questions.
   1   Where is Janet from? *She's from Nova Scotia, Canada.*
   2   What is Janet's job?
   ....
   3   Where does Janet work?
   ....
   4   Where does Janet go shopping on Saturday?
   ....
   5   What time does the market close on Sunday?
   ....
   6   What does Janet always buy on Sunday?
   ....
   7   Who does Janet meet on Sunday evening?
   ....
   8   What does Janet like?
   ....
   9   What does Janet love?
   ....

13 Now read the article again and check.

> **Learner tip**
>
> Read, read, read! Reading is a very good way to learn more English. You see and learn more words. Try reading these in English:
> – free newspapers and magazines
> – news on the internet
> – websites about things you are interested in
> – books for children or young adults

04

GRAMMAR Can ...?

1 🔊 **4.6 Listen and number the questions in the order you hear them.**
a Can you close the window? [ ]
b Can you do Exercises 4 and 5? [ ]
c Can we have food in the class? [ ]
d Can you wait ten minutes? [ ]
e Can we have a break? [ ]
f Can you help me? [ ]

2 Complete the questions with *Can I* or *Can you*.
1 I'm tired. *Can I* have a break?
2 This is difficult. .... help me?
3 .... do Exercises 4 and 5 for homework, please?
4 I don't have time to eat my sandwich. .... have five more minutes?
5 .... wait two minutes? I need to go to the toilet.
6 .... have my coffee in the class?

3 Write questions.
1 We can have a break.
   Can we have a break?
2 We can have ten more minutes.
   ....
3 We can't have food in the class.
   ....
4 You can close the window.
   ....
5 You can do Exercise 9.
   ....
6 You can help me.
   ....
7 You can wait a minute.
   ....

VOCABULARY Classroom verbs

4 Match the verbs 1–8 with a–h.
1 come   [*c*]   a the light
2 leave   [   ]   b at the front
3 play   [   ]   c in
4 share   [   ]   d your tablet
5 sit   [   ]   e it again
6 turn on   [   ]   f early
7 use   [   ]   g it on the board
8 write   [   ]   h your book

5 Complete the conversations with words from Exercise 4.
1 A: Can we have a break?
   B: No, but you can *leave* early.
2 A: I can't see my book!
   B: .... the light.
3 A: I'm late. Sorry.
   B: That's OK. .... in.
4 A: I don't understand. Can you .... it on the board?
   B: Sure.
5 A: I don't know this word.
   B: .... your tablet.
6 A: I don't have my book. Can you .... your book?
   B: OK.

DEVELOPING WRITING
A note describing where you live

> **Language note**
>
> When you write in English, you can use words like *and* and *but* to make two short sentences one long sentence.
> There's a church. There's a school. = There's a church **and** a school.
> There's a bus station. There isn't a train station. = There's a bus station, **but** there isn't a train station.

6 Complete the sentences with *and* or *but*.
1 I work late on Monday, ... I don't work on Tuesday.
2 There's a cash machine here, ... there isn't a bank.
3 I have a pen .... I have paper.
4 There's a park .... there's a supermarket.
5 My sister lives in a village, ... I live in a big town.
6 Jo goes to the café on Saturday morning .... meets her friends.

7 Read the note quickly and circle the correct answer.
1 Marcia's note is for:
   a her doctor
   b her father
   c her friend
2 The note is about:
   a work
   b places
   c school

Hi Juan,

Sorry I'm not here, but this is my flat – Flat 12, ¹ *20 Garden Road*! This is a nice area and I love it! There's a café on the corner and a restaurant next to the flat. There isn't a museum here, but you can ² .... to the centre. There's a ³ .... The City Museum. It normally opens ⁴ .... and it usually closes at 7 at night. It's always closed on Monday. There's a clothes shop ⁵ ...., but I always go shopping in the centre. There are lots of good clothes shops there. Have a great holiday!

Marcia

8 Complete Marcia's note to Juan with the phrases in the box.

~~20 Garden Road~~	at 10 in the morning
down the road	museum there called
take the train	

9 Complete the notes for your home.
This is my house/flat – ....
There's ....
It normally opens at .... and it usually closes at ....
It's always closed on ....
There isn't ....
You can take the .... to ....

10 Write a note for a friend who is going to stay in your home. Use your notes from Exercise 9. Use the model text in Exercise 7.

Vocabulary Builder Quiz 4

Download the Vocabulary Builder for Unit 4 and try the quiz below. Write your answers in your notebook. Then check them and record your score.

1 Circle the correct words.
1 **see**   night / a film
2 **need** $5 / shopping
3 **open**   a shop / a light
4 **study**   a market / English
5 **share**   your homework / your tablet

2 Write the words in the box in the correct place.

| machine | name | park | shop | station |

1 cash ....
2 train ....
3 clothes ....
4 car ....
5 family ....

3 Match the beginnings (1–5) with the endings (a–e).
1 What time do you get   a off the TV, please?
2 The school is next   b up every day?
3 Can you turn   c at the front of the room?
4 Is the teacher   d to the park.
5 Sorry, I'm late. Can I come e in, please?

4 Complete the groups with the words in the box.

| book | evening | mosque | third | today |

1 first   second   ....
2 church   religion   ....
3 morning   afternoon   ....
4 board   classroom   ....
5 yesterday   tomorrow   ....

5 Complete the words in the sentences.
1 How m........................... supermarkets are in this area?
2 The cinema is on the left and the bank is on the r...........................
3 Do you know a restaurant c........................... D'Angelos?
4 Oh, no! The supermarket is c...........................! I need milk and bread!
5 A: I don't u........................... this word.
   B: Use your dictionary.

Score ___/25

Wait a couple of weeks and try the quiz again. Compare your scores.

04 WHERE AND WHEN   119

05 GOING PLACES

VOCABULARY Getting there

1 Complete the table with the words in the box. Sometimes more than one answer is correct.

| a taxi | for the bus | home | off the train |
| the metro | the red line | to work | trains |

get	go	take
a taxi		

walk	change	wait

2 Complete the conversations with verbs from Exercise 1.
1 A: I work in an office on Scotland Road.
    B: How do you get there?
    A: I usually *get* a taxi or I sometimes .... on nice days.
2 A: Can you help me, please? I want to go to the main square.
    B: OK. .... the blue line and .... trains at Central Station.
3 A: I don't feel very well.
    B: Do you want to .... home? You can leave early.
4 A: I usually .... about ten minutes for the bus to school.
    B: Oh. I always .... the metro.
5 A: To get to my flat, ... off the train at Sloan Station.
    B: Can you say that again?
    A: Yes, Sloan Station.

Learner tip
When you learn new words, write them with the words they often go with. For example:
get off the bus, get a taxi
GET
get to work, get married

GRAMMAR Are there ... ? / There are ...

3 Choose the correct option (a, b or c).
A: Do you like my new flat, Jason?
B: Yes, it's great! ¹ .... any interesting places near here?
A: Yes, ² .... lots of good places. You like museums. ³ .... two interesting museums in this area.
B: Cool! And I want to go shopping. Are there ⁴ .... shops near here?
A: No, ⁵ .... shops, but ⁶ .... a great market in the Old Town.
B: ⁷ .... a café in the Old Town?
A: Yes, there's ⁸ .... café called Coffee Express. It's really nice. Do you want to go there?
B: Yes, I need a coffee!

1	a Is there	b There are	(c) Are there
2	a there are	b there's	c is there
3	a There's	b There are	c There aren't
4	a a	b some	c any
5	a there isn't	b there are no	c there are
6	a there's	b there are	c are there
7	a there's	b Is there	c Are there
8	a some	b a	c any

4 🔊 5.1 Listen and check your answers.

5 Correct the underlined mistakes in the sentences.
1 I'm hungry. ~~There are~~ any nice restaurants near here?
    Are there
2 I need some new clothes for the party. Is there <u>some</u> good clothes shop near here? ....
3 <u>There are</u> a new supermarket in my area. I want to go shopping there! ....
4 We want a coffee and a sandwich. <u>There is no</u> café on this road? ....
5 <u>There's</u> three or four interesting places in the Old Town. ....
6 I want to go on holiday in Barcelona. Are there <u>a</u> good hotels there? ....

6 Write sentences about where you live.
1 There's ....
2 There are ....
3 There isn't a ....

7 Write questions to ask a friend about where they live.
1 Is there a .... ?
2 Are there any .... ?

120 OUTCOMES

DEVELOPING CONVERSATIONS *best*

8 Write *best* in the correct place.

              best
1. It's far from here. It's ̭ to take a taxi.

2. Where's the place to see some interesting art?

3. What's the area in the city?

4. Is that the café to sit and have a coffee?

5. Where's the place to go swimming?

LISTENING

9 🔊 5.2 Listen to five conversations. Where do the people want to go? Match the photos (a–e) with the conversations (1–5).

Conversation 1   photo [*b*]
Conversation 2   photo [   ]
Conversation 3   photo [   ]
Conversation 4   photo [   ]
Conversation 5   photo [   ]

10 🔊 5.2 Listen again. Are the sentences true or false? Circle T or F.

1. There's a restaurant on North Road.   (T) F
2. There are some good cafés on North Road. T F
3. The market is in the city centre. T F
4. The supermarket is forty minutes from the village. T F
5. The cash machine is near the bank. T F
6. The cash machine is near a hospital. T F
7. The museum is called the City Museum. T F
8. There are fifteen museums on Gosposka Street. T F
9. The Old Square is a good place to have a walk. T F
10. There are no nice places near the Old Square. T F

Learner tip

Try to work with a friend to practise your English. Practise asking and answering questions like the ones in Exercises 4 and 5.

05

VOCABULARY Buying tickets

1 Complete the phrases with the vowels (a, e, i, o, u).
1 ch *a* ng *e* tr *a* i ns
2 p __ y by c __ rd
3 f __ rst cl __ ss
4 the n __ xt tr __ __ n
5 r __ t __ rn
6 s __ c __ nd cl __ ss
7 s __ ngl __

2 Look at the photos and complete the crossword.

Across →
2   4   5

Down ↓
1   3

3 Circle the correct words.
1 Excuse me. Can you help me? Where do I *enter* / *change* trains for Covent Garden?
2 You can *buy* / *pay* by cash or *card* / *ticket*.
3 The best way to go is *first class* / *second class*, but it's expensive.
4 I need a bus ticket. Can I use that *cash* / *machine*?
5 Put your card in here and *enter* / *pay* your number.
6 I need a ticket, please – a *return* / *single*. I'm back tomorrow.
7 Hello there. Is the *next* / *single* train at 9.32?
8 Thank you. And here is your *receipt* / *machine*.

PRONUNCIATION /k/ and /s/

4 Read these words and think about the sound of the letters in bold. What are the two different sounds?

card	**c**ash	**c**entre	**c**ity
costs	first **c**lass	offi**c**e	re**c**eipt

5 🔊 5.3 Listen and write the words.

/k/   /s/
card   ....
....
....
....

Language note

The letter *c* has the sound /k/ before a consonant or vowels *a*, *o* and *u*, but /s/ before vowels *e*, *i*, *y*.

6 🔊 5.3 Listen again and repeat.

READING

7 Read the three adverts for bus trips. Which advert talks about how many people you travel with? Tick (✓) the correct answer.

Advert 1   [ ]
Advert 2   [ ]
Advert 3   [ ]

8 Circle the correct answers.
Advert 1
1 a You can visit nine other places.
  b You can visit twelve other places.
2 a A return costs £1,230.
  b A single costs $1,640.
Advert 2
3 a You sleep on the bus.
  b You sleep in hotels.
4 a There are twelve passengers on the bus.
  b There are fifteen passengers on the bus.
Advert 3
5 a You travel only to Lima.
  b You travel to Lima and Cusco.
6 a You can get off the bus.
  b You can't get off the bus.

9 Now read the adverts again and check.

FIRST CLASS TRIPS
Buses are cheap and they are the best! Take the bus!

❶ **Take the bus** from London and visit nine different cities in Europe. Sleep in great hotels and eat in the best restaurants! The trip takes twelve days and a return ticket costs £1,230 ($1,640). You can sit and see the world outside. You can get great views from the bus. You can see Paris, and the beautiful mountains in Switzerland and Italy.

❷ **Take the bus** from Helsinki to Berlin. The journey takes five days. You sleep in hotels and you can get off and visit lots of interesting places. There are only twelve passengers on the bus. You can sit and talk together. It only costs $450!

❸ **Take the bus** and see Peru in South America. Have a walk down the streets of Lima. Sit and have a coffee in the afternoon or have dinner in the evening in the main square of Cusco. The trip takes eight days. That's a lot of time to make friends! It costs £2,095. Have a great trip!

DEVELOPING CONVERSATIONS
Where are you going?

10 5.4 **Where are the people going? Listen and match the conversations (1–5) to the places (a–e).**

Conversation 1	[d]	a to Cannes
Conversation 2	[ ]	b to the main square
Conversation 3	[ ]	c to Berlin
Conversation 4	[ ]	d to Truro
Conversation 5	[ ]	e to the Old Town

05 GOING PLACES 123

GRAMMAR
Talking about plans: *I'm / We're going*

1 Look at the underlined words in the sentences. Write them in the correct column in the table.

Where	What	When
to the bank		

1 We're going to the bank after the class.
2 I'm going to the market this afternoon.
3 I'm going to have dinner with Lucy this evening.
4 We're going to meet friends now.
5 I'm going to see some interesting art tonight.
6 We're going to the museum tomorrow.
7 We're going to go swimming on Sunday.
8 I'm going home at five.

2 Complete the sentences with *'m going* or *'re going*.
1 I *'m going* to play football at five.
2 Dom and I – we .... to the supermarket on Saturday.
3 We .... to have a walk after work.
4 I .... to the park this afternoon.
5 I .... to bed now.
6 We .... to see a film tomorrow.

3 Complete the sentences with *'m going to* or *'re going to* and a verb from the box.

| eat | have | meet | play | see | stay |

1 I .... football this afternoon with some friends.
2 We .... a coffee after the class.
3 I .... my sister in town tomorrow.
4 Do you want to come to the cinema? We .... Ocean's 8.
5 I'm hungry. I .... my sandwich.
6 We .... at home and watch a film tonight.

4 Complete the sentences for you.
1 Tonight I ....
2 Tomorrow I ....
3 At the weekend I ....
4 Next week I ....

GRAMMAR
Asking about plans: *going* and *doing*

5 Complete the sentences with *going* or *doing*.
1 Where are you *going*?
2 Are you .... to the café?
3 What are you .... this evening?
4 What time are you ....?
5 What are you .... on Monday?

6 Complete the conversations with the questions in the box.

| Are you going | What are you doing |
| What time are you going | Where are you going |

1 A: I'm going to go shopping at two.
   B: .... ?
   A: The clothes shop on Bayer's Road.
2 A: I'm going to London on Sunday. Do you want to come?
   B: .... ?
   A: Nine or ten in the morning.
3 A: Are you going to the gym tonight?
   B: Yes. .... , too?
   A: Yes. Do you want to share a taxi?
4 A: .... after the class?
   B: I'm going to the cinema. Do you want to come?
   A: Sorry. I can't. I'm going to stay here.

DEVELOPING WRITING
Writing a text message

Language note

Nouns are words like *ticket*, *Marie* and *Tom*.
Pronouns are words like *it*, *she*, *he* and *they*.
When you write, try not to use the same nouns again and again – use pronouns.
Here's your ticket. ~~Your ticket~~ It *is a single.*
I'm going to meet Tom. ~~Tom~~ He *is my brother.*

7 Circle the correct option.
1 I'm going to the gym with Karim. *He / It* works in my office.
2 There's a ticket machine in the train station. *It's / She's* next to platform 5.
3 I'm going to go shopping with Lily. *It's / She's* my friend.
4 I'm going to the museum with Brad and Lee. *He / They* are my brothers.

124 OUTCOMES

8 Complete the sentences with the pronouns in the box.

| He | It | She | They |

1 I'm going on holiday with Jane. ....'s my sister.
2 I'm going to sit and have lunch with Sebastian. ....'s my son.
3 I'm going to share a taxi with Bridget and Liam. .... are married.
4 There's a bank on this street. ....'s on the corner.

9 Read the text quickly. What is it?
a a blog   b a text message   c a letter

Hi, Lydia. What are you doing ¹ *tonight*? I'm going to ² .... in town with my friend, Karim. We're going to see ³ .... – it's a great film. Do you want to come? To get to the cinema, take ⁴ .... It's the blue line. Get off at Victoria Station. I'll meet you outside the cinema at ⁵ ....

10 Now complete the text with the phrases in the box.

| Deadpool 2 | eight | the cinema |
| the metro | ~~tonight~~ | |

11 Make plans to do something with a friend. Complete the notes.
I'm going to .... (what?) .... (where?) .... (when?).
I'm going with .... (who?).
To get to .... (what?), take .... (how?)
Get off .... (where?).
I'll meet you .... (where?) at .... (what time?).

12 Write a text message to a friend. Use your notes from Exercise 11. Use the model text in Exercise 9.

05

Vocabulary Builder Quiz 5

Download the Vocabulary Builder for Unit 5 and try the quiz below. Write your answers in your notebook. Then check them and record your score.

1 Circle the correct words.
1 I'm going to the cinema at three *later / o'clock*.
2 You can see the world *outside / there* on a bus trip.
3 Can I pay by *receipt / cash*?
4 There are some cafés in the *cheap / main* square.
5 How many *passengers / parties* are going to Liverpool?

2 Put the letters in the correct order and write the words.
1 How long is your (liftgh) .... to Rome?
2 Take the red (neil) .... and change at Victoria station.
3 Can I have a (tunrer) ...., please? I'm back on Monday.
4 We had a good holiday in Australia, but it was a long (ojneyur) ....
5 We're going to see a lot of beautiful (wsvei) .... on our holiday.

3 Circle the incorrect words.
1 **sleep**   well   every   at night
2 **get off**   second class   at the park   the train
3 **get**   to my house   here   a long time
4 **talk**   work   about a trip   to friends
5 **put**   your bag there   money in the machine   some help

4 Complete the sentences with the words in the box.

| card | football | home | museum | platform |

1 I'm sorry, but I want to stay at .... tonight.
2 I want to buy a ticket. Can I pay by ....?
3 Do you want to play .... next weekend?
4 I'm going to visit a .... in the Old Town.
5 A: We're going to Leeds.
   B: OK. Wait on .... 12.

5 Match the beginnings (1–5) with the endings (a–e).
1 Don't take a bus. You can take
2 It's the break. Are you going to eat
3 A ticket to Southsea costs
4 Please enter
5 Do you want to share

a £10.
b your number here.
c a sandwich?
d the metro.
e a taxi to the airport?

Score ___/25

Wait a couple of weeks and try the quiz again.
Compare your scores.

06 AWAY FROM HOME

VOCABULARY Problems

1 Label the photos. Put the letters in the correct order and write the words.

1 eatl *late*
2 nseoi ....
3 inra ....
4 on-neo ....
5 retid ....
6 ffictra ....

2 Circle the correct word.
1 A: Is that Jane's flat?
   B: No, we're in the right area, but we're in the (wrong) / tired road!
2 A: There's a lot of *noise / traffic* today.
   B: Yes, and it's all going to the city centre!
3 A: What's that *problem / noise* outside our room?
   B: I don't know, but I can't sleep.
4 A: Is there a lot of *rain / traffic* in London?
   B: Yes, and I don't like it. I like hot weather.
5 A: We need to buy our train tickets.
   B: Yes, but there's *nowhere / no-one* here to help us.
6 A: Are you *tired / late*, Stephan?
   B: Yes, I want to go to bed.
7 A: We're going to the cinema this evening. Do you want to come?
   B: Sorry, I need to work *wrong / late*.
8 A: The train is very busy.
   B: Yes, and there's *no-one / nowhere* to sit.
9 A: I have *a problem / rain* at the office.
   B: Oh, do you need to work this evening?

Learner tip

Write different sentences with the new words you learn, or practise using new words in conversation with a classmate or another English speaker/learner. You need to use a new word about ten to fifteen times before you remember it.

GRAMMAR Past simple: irregular verbs

3 Complete the table with the past simple form of the verbs.

Present simple	Past simple
(be) is	1 *was*
(be) are	2
have / has	3
go / goes	4
do / does	5

4 Complete the sentences with the verbs in brackets. Use the past simple.
1 We *were* (be) late for the party yesterday.
2 I'm tired. I .... (have) a lot of problems at the office today.
3 My friends .... (go) to China on their last holiday.
4 Sorry, I'm late. There .... (be) a lot of traffic.
5 It .... (be) a great trip! We .... (do) a lot of things and we .... (go) to a lot of interesting places.
6 I .... (be) wrong about the flight number last week. Sorry!
7 I .... (do) a lot of work this morning.

126 OUTCOMES

Developing conversations
Don't worry / That's OK

5 🔊 **6.1 Complete the conversations with the words in the box. Listen and check your answers.**

Don't	OK	~~That~~	That's	worry

1. A: Hi, Maria. Sorry, I'm late.
   B: *That*'s OK. How was your journey?
2. A: I don't have any money for lunch.
   B: .... worry. I have some.
3. A: Sorry, I'm late. I went to the wrong flat.
   B: That's .... You're here now!
4. A: I can't come to the cinema. I had a problem at home.
   B: Don't .... We can go tomorrow.
5. A: I don't have my English book.
   B: .... OK. You can share my book.

Reading

6 Read the email quickly. Where did Berat and his brother go on holiday? Tick the correct answer.
   a Ankara [ ]   b Barcelona [ ]   c Japan [ ]

7 Are the sentences true or false? Circle T or F.
1. The journey from Ankara to Barcelona was good, but it was long. (T) F
2. Berat and his brother were only on one plane. T F
3. Their room was expensive. T F
4. They did a lot of things on their holiday. T F
5. La Rambla had no noise or traffic. T F
6. It was hot, but there was rain. T F

8 Circle the correct words.
1. Berat and his brother are from *Spain / (Turkey)*.
2. Their journey was *six hours and thirty minutes / six hours and thirteen minutes*.
3. Their hotel was in *La Rambla / Via Laietana*.
4. *Via Laietana / La Rambla* had a lot of interesting places on it.
5. They went to a swimming pool near their hotel every *evening / morning*.

9 Now read the email again and check.

[Sent] [Chat] [Attach] [Font]

Hi Siobhan,

How are you? My brother and I had a great trip to Spain. The journey from Ankara, in Turkey, to Barcelona was good, but it was long – six hours and thirty minutes. We changed planes in Munich, Germany.

Our hotel in the city was called Hotel Colonial Barcelona. It was in a busy street called Via Laietana. Our room was expensive – $103 for one night, but it was a good hotel in the best area of the city.

We did a lot of things on our holiday. We went to a road in the city centre called La Rambla. It had some interesting places on it. It had cafés, restaurants and places to go shopping. It was nice, but there was a lot of noise and traffic.

The weather was great. It was hot and there was no rain! We went to a swimming pool near our hotel every evening.

Well, it's late and I'm tired now. I want to go to bed! How was your holiday in Japan?

Write soon,
Berat

06 AWAY FROM HOME 127

06

VOCABULARY Hotels and checking in

1 Circle the correct words to label the pictures.

1 check out / booking
2 number / bag
3 lift / room
4 breakfast / passport
5 key / password
6 lift / booking
7 address / password
8 breakfast / passport

2 Complete the sentences with words from Exercise 1.
1 My *address* is 26 Seaview Road, Flat .... 4.
2 Do you have your .... ? You need it to get on the plane!
3 We want to have .... in the morning before we .... of the hotel.
4 Here's the .... for your room. It's room 258, on the second floor.
5 The .... is over there – you don't need to use the stairs.
6 We have a .... for two nights. My name is Ahmed Asfour.
7 We want to use the WiFi. What's the .... ?
8 Can you help me with my .... , please? It's very big!

GRAMMAR Regular past simple endings

Language note

Most regular verbs add *-ed* in the past simple.
work > work**ed**   want > want**ed**

Regular verbs that end in an *e* add *-d* in the past simple.
liv**e** > liv**ed**   us**e** > us**ed**

3 Complete the table with the past simple form of the verbs in the box.

| like | love | rain | share | stay | talk |

verb + -d	verb + -ed
liked	

4 Complete the sentences with the verbs in brackets. Use the past simple.
1 We *liked* (like) the local food.
2 I .... (stay) in a five-star hotel in Belfast.
3 It .... (rain) every day on my holiday.
4 We .... (love) the café in our hostel in Cuba.
5 Mr Smith .... (talk) to my mother yesterday.
6 I .... (share) a room with my sister on holiday.

128 OUTCOMES

PRONUNCIATION Past simple forms

5 🔊 **6.2** Listen to these past simple forms. Do the letters in bold sound the same or different? Write the words in the correct column of the table.

lik**ed**	rain**ed**	visit**ed**
/t/	/d/	/ɪd/
liked		

6 🔊 **6.3** Listen to these past forms and write them in the correct column of the table in Exercise 5.

danced	needed	shared	started	stayed
talked	walked	wanted	watched	

7 🔊 **6.3** Listen again and repeat.

GRAMMAR Past simple negatives

8 Write the past negative form of the verbs.
1 had   *didn't have*
2 liked   ....
3 rained   ....
4 saw   ....
5 talked   ....
6 was   ....
7 went   ....
8 were   ....
9 did   ....

9 Make the sentences negative.
1 It rained in my city on Friday.
   It didn't rain in my city on Friday.
2 On my trip, I saw interesting art.
   ....
3 At school, I talked to my English teacher.
   ....
4 I had a party last weekend.
   ....
5 On my holiday, I liked the local food.
   ....
6 I did a lot of work today.
   ....
7 On my bus journey, there was a lot of noise.
   ....
8 I went shopping yesterday.
   ....

10 Tick the sentences in Exercise 9 that are true for you.

LISTENING

11 🔊 **6.4** Listen to the conversation between Chang and his wife. Why is Chang late home from work? Tick (✓) the correct picture.

1 ☐

2 ☐

3 ☐

12 Match the sentence beginnings (1–9) with the endings (a–i).
1 There was   [*f*]   a no-one to help me.
2 How was   [   ]   b work?
3 It wasn't   [   ]   c very big.
4 The shop was very busy,   d lunch this afternoon.
   but there was   [   ]   e to bed late last night.
5 Yes, I didn't have   [   ]   f a lot of traffic in the
6 I didn't like   [   ]   centre.
7 It wasn't   [   ]   g a lot of work today
8 I did   [   ]   and I'm tired.
9 I went   [   ]   h very good.
                                   i that restaurant.

13 🔊 **6.4** Listen again and check your answers.

06 AWAY FROM HOME   129

06

GRAMMAR
Past simple questions

1 Circle the correct words.
1. What *did you have* / *did you had* for lunch today?
2. Where *went you* / *did you go* on holiday last year?
3. What time *did you leave* / *you did leave* for work/school this morning?
4. What films *were you saw* / *did you see* last week?
5. What time *did you get* / *did you got* to work/school this morning?
6. *Did you go* / *Went you* out last Saturday night?
7. What *did you* / *did you do* last weekend?
8. *Did you went* / *Did you go* shopping yesterday?

2 Write true answers to the questions in Exercise 1.

3 Complete the questions with *you* and the past simple form of the verbs in the box. Then match the questions (1–6) with the answers (a–f).

~~buy~~ get up go live stay study

1. What **did you buy** at the shops yesterday?
2. Where .... in 2015? A house or a flat?
3. Where .... last night?
4. What time .... this morning?
5. What .... at university?
6. .... at home every day last week?

a In a flat. [ ]
b No, only on Monday, Wednesday and Friday. [ ]
c Some clothes and a bag. [1]
d To the gym. [ ]
e At seven. [ ]
f English. [ ]

GRAMMAR REVIEW: Past simple

4 Put the words in the correct order.
1. at the café / was / there / a problem
   There was a problem at the café.
2. for class / weren't / we / late
3. had / at home / I / breakfast
4. to the museum / didn't / they / go
5. a lot of / we / interesting things / did
6. ? / get / you / home / did / when
7. like / I / Rome / didn't

8. a great hostel / we / in / stayed
9. ? / you / the doctor / did / talk to
10. ? / you / did / dinner / where / have

5 Complete the conversations with the words in brackets. Use the correct past simple form.
1. A: Why are you late?
   B: Sorry. The weather **was** (be) very bad.
2. A: Why are you tired?
   B: I .... (go) to bed late last night.
3. A: What .... (you / have) for lunch?
   B: I .... (not have) lunch –
      I .... (be) very busy.
4. A: Where .... (you / stay) in Peru?
   B: We .... (stay) in Lima.
5. A: How .... (be) the restaurant?
   B: Good. There .... (not be) a lot of people there.
6. A: .... (you / like) the hostel?
   B: No, we .... (share) a bathroom with ten other people!
7. A: What .... (you / see) at the museum yesterday?
   B: We .... (not go) to the museum.
      We .... (walk) around the Old Town.

DEVELOPING WRITING
Writing a review

> **Language note**
>
> When you write in English, always watch your spelling. Some words sound the same, but have different spelling and meaning.
>
> *I went **to** Indonesia.*
> *I saw **two** lakes.*
>
> *I went **there** in December.*
> *They had lunch with **their** mother.*
>
> ***We're** in our rooms.*
> *The rooms **were** nice.*

6 Circle the correct words.
1. We went *to* / *two* South Africa on our holiday.
2. They did lots of things with *there* / *their* friends.
3. The views *were* / *we're* great.
4. We saw *to* / *two* markets in the Old Town.
5. *Were* / *We're* at the hostel.
6. I went *there* / *their* by plane.

06

7 Read the review quickly and circle the correct answer.
The review is for:
a a country   b a holiday   c a hotel

journeyadvice — Bali

Tell us about your holiday in Bali. We're waiting for your reviews!

Bali Green Hostel
★★★★

I stayed in a hostel called the Bali Green Hostel for five days and I shared a room with six other people. The room cost $16 for one night. I went to the hostel very late at night, but that wasn't a problem. There was someone there – he worked all night. My room was very clean and my bed was new. There were towels and soap in the bathroom. The hostel didn't have a restaurant, but it had a café. The food and service were good and the café wasn't expensive. The hostel was near a supermarket and a beautiful beach. I did some interesting things in Bali. One day, I went on a trip to Kuta with some new friends. I saw a very old temple there. I had lunch at a nice restaurant and talked to lots of local people. Another day I went shopping at a market. I loved my holiday!

8 Write a review of a holiday. Complete the notes.
I went to .... on my holiday.
I stayed in a .... for .... days.
I didn't share / shared a .... with ....
The room cost .... for ....
My room was .... and ....
There were .... and .... in the ....
The .... didn't have ...., but it had ....
The .... was near .... and ....
One day, I went ....
Another day I ....

9 Write a review of a holiday. Use your notes from Exercise 8 and the model review in Exercise 7. Remember to check your spelling.

Vocabulary Builder Quiz 6

Download the Vocabulary Builder for Unit 6 and try the quiz below. Write your answers in your notebook. Then check them and record your score.

1 Circle the correct words.
1 I like modern *music / noise*. Katy Perry is my favourite singer.
2 It's late. There's *nowhere / no-one* in my office.
3 Great to see you! How was your *plane / flight*?
4 Hi, my room number is 12. Can I have the WiFi *password / address*, please?
5 Did you like your *tour / journey* of London?

2 Complete the words in the sentences.
1 Sorry, I'm late. There was a lot of t .... in the city.
2 I didn't have breakfast and now I'm really h ....
3 Hi, my name is Janet Dean. I have a b .... for two nights.
4 A: Do you like this song?
   B: Yes, that's my favourite b .... !
5 A: Here's our room. Oh, no! Where's our k .... ?
   B: It's OK. I have it in my bag.

3 Circle the incorrect words.
1 **a busy**   party   gym   city centre
2 **clean**   the bathroom   your bed   the car
3 **have**   dinner   lunch   exercise
4 **last**   weather   night   year
5 **a quiet**   time of day   problem   hostel

4 Complete the sentences with the words in the box.

| lake | lift | passport | rain | star |

1 I need a .... I'm going to China next year.
2 It's a five-................ hotel. It's expensive, but very nice.
3 Our hotel was near a .... We went swimming every day!
4 We get lots of .... in London.
5 Your room is on the third floor. You can use the .... over there.

5 Match the beginnings (1–5) with the endings (a–e).
1 How was your holiday? Did you stay
2 I'm very tired. I want to sleep
3 Hello, Mr Peters. Can you sign
4 Did you meet
5 I'm going to watch

a here, please?
b in a nice hotel?
c a film tonight.
d for one or two hours.
e any interesting people in Rome?

Score ___/25

Wait a couple of weeks and try the quiz again. Compare your scores.

AUDIOSCRIPT

Unit 1

1.1
three
five
six
nine
eleven
twelve

1.2
E = Ethan, I = Ines, K = Khalid
I: What's your name?
K: Khalid.
I: Hi. I'm Ines.
K: Nice to meet you.
I: Yes. You, too.
K: Ines, this is my friend Ethan.
I: Hi. Nice to meet you.
E: Yes. You, too, Ines.

1.3
H = Hugh, L = Liam, R= Rebeca, S = Shirley
1 S: Liam is my husband. He's a doctor.
2 L: Shirley is my wife. She's a teacher in an English school. This is my son, Hugh. He's nine. And she is my daughter, Rebeca. She's nine, too!
3 R: Hugh's my brother. He is my best friend, too. We're in the same class at school!
4 H: Rebeca is my sister. My mother is a teacher and my father is a doctor.

1.4
four
eight
twelve
fifteen
nineteen
twenty
twenty-two

1.5
1 thirty
2 eighteen
3 nineteen dollars ninety-nine
4 fourteen
5 seven euros fifty

1.6
A: What would you like?
B: How much is a small orange juice?
A: Three ninety-nine.
B: OK. A small orange juice, please.
A: Orange juice. Anything else?
B: Yes – a coffee cake, please.
A: OK. Anything else?
B: No, thanks.
A: That's seven ninety-nine.

1.7
A: Hi, what would you like, sir?
B: How much is a large latte?
A: Four fifty.
B: OK. A large latte, please.
A: Anything else?
B: Yes – a chocolate cake, please.
A: Thank you!
 ... Here you are. Is everything OK?
B: No. My latte – it's not right.
A: What's the problem, sir?
B: This is a small latte – not a large.
A: Oh, yes. Sorry. OK. That's nine ninety.

Unit 2

2.1
A = Angelina, S = Sebastian
S: Hi. Sorry. What's your name?
A: Angelina. And you?
S: Sebastian. Nice to meet you.
A: You, too.
S: So, Angelina. Where do you live?
A: I live on Venice Road. Do you know it?
S: Yes. It's near our school, right?
A: Yes. I walk here. It takes ten minutes.
S: Nice!
A: And you? Where do you live, Sebastian?
S: Westville. It's a small village. Do you know it?
A: No. Is it far?
S: It takes twenty minutes by bus.
A: Do you live in a house or a flat?
S: I live in a small flat with two friends. And you?
A: I live in a big house with my mother and father.

2.2
W= waiter, C1 = customer 1, C2 = customer 2
W: Are you ready to order?
C1: Yes. A burger with chips for me.
W: And you?
C2: The fish, please.
W: With rice or chips?
C2: Chips, please.
W: Anything else with your fish?
C2: How much is a salad?
W: It's ten pounds.
C2: Oh! No, thanks.

2.3
1
M = man, W = woman
M: I love espresso!
W: I don't like it. I only like tea.
2
B = boy, W = woman
B: I don't like vegetables, Mum!
W: Oh, Tommy! You only like cakes and ice cream!
B: I love cakes and ice cream!

132 OUTCOMES

3

M = man, W = waiter

M Do you have a table for three?
W: Yes. Would you like a menu in English?
M: Yes, please.

4

M = man, W = waiter

W: Would you like a drink, sir?
M: How much is a coke?
W: Five euros thirty.
M: Oh. It's expensive. No, thanks.

2.4

bus driver
doctors
does
flats
hours
house
lives
south

Unit 3

3.1

1 an expensive flat
2 an orange bus
3 an English teacher
4 an old village

3.2

1
A: How's your son?
B: He's not very well.
A: Oh, no! I'm sorry.
B: How's your daughter?
A: She's great!
B: Good.

2
C: How's your flat?
D: It's good, but flats in the city are expensive.
C: Yes!

3
E: How's the weather?
F: It's very hot. I love it.
E: Oh. It's not normally hot in Canada.

4
G: How's your job?
H: It's not very good. How's *your* job?
G: The same. And it's difficult!
H: Yeah, I know.

3.3

B = Bandile, E = Emma

E: Where are you from, Bandile?
B: Buenos Aires.
E: Sorry? Can you say that again?
B: Buenos Aires, in Argentina.
E: Great. Welcome to London! Are you tired?
B: Sorry. Can you say that again?
E: Are you tired?
B: Er … yes. I'm hot and tired. I need to take a shower.
E: Oh, yes. Of course. Do you want anything?
B: Do you have … er, … for my shower …
E: A towel?
B: No, I have a towel. I need some … er, *seep*. How do you say *seep* in English?
E: Soap!

Unit 4

4.1

A: Is there a restaurant near here?
B: No, there isn't.
A: OK. Is there a café? I'm very hungry!
B: No, sorry, there isn't one on this road.
A: Oh. Is there a supermarket?
B: Yes, there's one next to the cinema! They have sandwiches.

4.2

1 A: Do you know a town called Southsea?
　 B: No, is it far?
2 On Park Road, there's a clothes shop called Nice and New. I often go shopping there.
3 There's a nice restaurant called Angelo's near my house. It has great pizza!
4 A: There's a cinema called the Odeon there.
　 B: Yes, do you want to see a film?
5 A: Do you know a café called The CoffeeShop?
　 B: Yes, it's very expensive.

4.3

1
A: Excuse me. Do you know a café called the Big Cappuccino on this road?
B: Er … No, I don't. I don't know the town.
A: Oh, OK.
B: There are some cafés near here, but I don't know their names.
A: Oh.
B: Walk down this road. I think there's a café at the end.
A: Oh, yes – it is at the end of a road!
B: Maybe that's it. Down on the left; next to the park.
A: Yes, maybe. Thank you.

AUDIOSCRIPT

2
C: Hello. Excuse me.
D: Hello.
C: Is there a cash machine near here?
D: A cash machine ... No, there isn't a cash machine, but there's a bank on Maple Road. Down there. The first on the left.
C: Sorry, can you say that again?
D: Sorry. Down there. The first road. Go left.
C: The second road?
D: No, the first road. It's a big road called Maple Road. The bank is on the right.
C: Oh, great! Thank you!

3
E: Hello, excuse me. Excuse me.
F: Hi. Sorry. Yes.
E: Is there a swimming pool near here?
F: A swimming pool ... er... yes. There's one down there.
E: How far is it?
F: Er ... I don't know – 250 metres? It's near a hospital called St Ann's.
E: OK – near the hospital.
F: Yes – St Ann's is on the corner, on the right, and the swimming pool is on the left.
E: OK. Thanks.

4.4
bank
station
hospital
market
supermarket
church

4.5
station
hospital
market
supermarket

4.6
1 A: Can you wait ten minutes?
   B: Sorry, I can't.
2 A: I don't know what floor my classroom is on. Can you help me?
   B: Sure!
3 A: This is difficult. Can we have a break?
   B: OK.
4 A: Do we have homework?
   B: Yes. Can you do Exercises 4 and 5?
5 A: We're cold.
   B: OK. Can you close the window?
6 A: Can we have food in the class?
   B: No, you can't.

Unit 5

5.1
J= Jason, W = Woman
W: Do you like my new flat, Jason?
J: Yes, it's great! Are there any interesting places near here?
W: Yes, there are lots of good places. You like museums. There are two interesting museums in this area.
J: Cool! And I want to go shopping. Are there any shops near here?
W: No, there are no shops, but there's a great market in the Old Town.
J: Is there a café in the Old Town?
W: Yes, there's a café called Coffee Express. It's really nice. Do you want to go there?
J: Yes, I need a coffee!

5.2
1
A: Hello there. Are there any places to sit and have lunch near here?
B: Not on this road. There's a restaurant on North Road, but the best place is the Old Town. There are some good cafés there.
A: Great, thanks!

2
C: I want to go shopping this afternoon. Where's the best place to go?
D: Well, there's a supermarket in the city centre. It's about forty minutes from here. But there's a market here, in the village. It's very good. Lots of people go there.

3
E: Excuse me. I need to get some money. Are there any banks on this road?
F: No, there are no banks, but there's a cash machine. It's near the hospital.

4
G: Is there a good museum near here? I want to go somewhere interesting this afternoon.
H: Yes. There are lots of interesting places. Try the City Museum. It's on a street called Gosposka. Number 15.

5
I: I want to have a walk. Where's the best place to go?
J: Try the area round the Old Square. I walk there every day. There are lots of nice places to see and the main square is great.

5.3
card
cash
centre
city
costs
first class
office
receipt

5.4

1
A: Where are you going?
B: To a town called Truro.
A: Oh. Is it far?

2
C: Where are you going?
D: To a city in France – Cannes.
C: Cool!

3
E: Where are you going?
F: To the Old Town – it's an interesting place.
E: Yes, I love it.

4
G: Where are you going?
H: To the main square. I want to sit and have a coffee.
G: Can I come?

5
I: Where are you going?
J: To Berlin.
I: Single or return?

Unit 6

6.1

1 A: Hi, Maria. Sorry, I'm late.
   B: That's OK. How was your journey?
2 A: I don't have any money for lunch.
   B: Don't worry. I have some.
3 A: Sorry, I'm late. I went to the wrong flat.
   B: That's OK. You're here now!
4 A: I can't come to the cinema. I had a problem at home.
   B: Don't worry. We can go tomorrow.
5 A: I don't have my English book.
   B: That's OK. You can share my book.

6.2
liked
rained
visited

6.3
danced
needed
shared
started
stayed
talked
walked
wanted
watched

6.4
C = Chang, M= Mia
M: Hi, Chang.
C: Hi, Mia. How are you?
M: Good, thanks.
C: Sorry, I'm late. I had a problem in the city. There was a lot of traffic in the centre.
M: That's OK – I know. It was on TV. How was work?
C: It wasn't very good. The shop was very busy, but there was no-one to help me.
M: Oh, I'm sorry. Are you hungry?
C: Yes, I didn't have lunch this afternoon. What are we doing this evening?
M: We're going to that restaurant on South Street.
C: Oh. I didn't like that restaurant. It wasn't very big and there were a lot of people there.
M: Don't worry. Do you want to stay at home?
C: Is that OK? I did a lot of work today and I'm tired.
M: Of course! I can get a pizza.
C: OK, good. Sorry, Mia. I went to bed late last night. I want to go to bed early tonight.

ANSWER KEY

UNIT 1
Vocabulary Numbers 1–12
1

G	J	T	F	I	V	E	U	J	G
G	S	W	E	E	T	J	S	X	I
A	B	E	J	Y	H	E	E	S	S
G	F	L	Q	K	R	K	L	T	I
O	V	V	K	S	E	V	E	N	X
D	F	E	H	O	E	F	V	W	T
G	T	W	O	O	N	E	E	I	E
T	C	Z	N	B	N	I	N	E	N
J	F	O	U	R	E	I	G	H	T
A	E	Y	X	K	R	H	G	C	Z

2
Students should circle: 3, 5, 6, 9, 11, 12

Listening
3
Picture 2

4
Ines, this is my friend Ethan. 6
Hi. I'm Ines. 3
Hi. Nice to meet you. 7
Khalid. 2
Nice to meet you. 4
What's your name? 1
Yes. You, too, Ines. 8
Yes. You, too. 5

Developing conversations Checking names
5
1 he   2 She's   3 they   4 I

6
1 I   3 's he   5 know
2 's she   4 are they   6 Who

Vocabulary People
7
1 doctor   3 friend   5 mother
2 teacher   4 son   6 wife

8
1 father   3 brother 5 sister
2 daughter   4 husband

9
1 husband   3 brother, friend
2 teacher, daughter   4 mother, father

Grammar 'm, 's, 're
10
1 's   2 'm   3 's   4 's   5 're   6 is   7 're   8 're

11
1 We're   2 He's   3 She's   4 I'm   5 They're

Vocabulary Numbers 13–22
1
18 ⑮ 21 ④ 17 ㉒ 13 16
14 3 10 ⑫ ⑲ ⑧ ⑳ 9

3
wz (fourteen) zst (eighteen) hj (twenty) ox (thirteen) vx (fifteen) uh (seventeen) mn (twenty-two) vu (sixteen) op (nineteen) nh (twenty-one)

Vocabulary Question words
4
1 What time   3 How much   5 Where
2 How old   4 Who   6 How long

5
1 Where   3 How long   5 How old
2 What time   4 How much   6 Who

Grammar Questions with be
6
1 are   3 is   5 Are   7 is
2 is   4 is   6 are   8 Are

7
1 What time is the break?   5 Who is he?
2 How much are the books?   6 Where is Akemi from?
3 How are you?   7 How old is Ava?
4 Is the coffee nice?   8 How long are the classes?

8
a 8   b 4   c 5   d 6   e 1   f 2   g 3   h 7

Grammar his, her, our, their
9
1 c   2 b   3 a   4 d

10
1 our   2 his   3 their   4 her

11
1 her   3 their   5 our
2 Ethan's   4 Sharon's

Reading
12
1 c   2 a   3 b

13
1 T   2 F   3 F   4 T   5 F   6 T

14
1 How long; three hours
2 What; 4pm–7pm
3 What; Friday
4 Who; Morgan and Sian's older son
5 How; She's 21.
6 Where's; a restaurant / Sam's Restaurant / 18 Brown Street

Vocabulary Times and prices
1
eighty   forty   thirty-two
fifty-seven   seventy   twenty
ninety-six   sixty-three

2
1 T   2 P   3 P   4 T   5 T   6 P

136 OUTCOMES

PRONUNCIATION Numbers
3
1 b   2 b   3 a   4 a   5 b

VOCABULARY In a coffee shop
5
1 sandwich   3 tea   5 large
2 cake   4 small

DEVELOPING CONVERSATIONS Ordering and serving drinks
6
1 would   3 much   5 Anything
2 like   4 else   6 thanks

GRAMMAR *not*
8
1 My sandwich – it's **not** right.
2 It's **not** a chocolate cake.
3 It's small – **not** medium.
4 My cappuccino – it's **not** hot.
5 A latte is $3.69 – **not** $5.69!

9
1 It's not right.
2 It's not small.
3 It's not a coffee cake.
4 It's not five pounds.
5 My americano is not hot.

LISTENING
10
b

11
1 Hi   3 Four fifty   5 large
2 latte   4 small   6 nine ninety

12
2 and 4

DEVELOPING WRITING Describing people
13
1 **C**ome to our party at 3 **H**igh **S**treet.
2 **T**his is my daughter, **P**oppy.
3 **H**i, I'm **L**ara.
4 **H**e's from **ã** **P**aulo in **B**razil.
5 **T**his is our son, **D**avid.

14
1, 3, 5, 6, 7, 8

VOCABULARY BUILDER QUIZ 1
1
1 D   2 F   3 F   4 D   5 F   6 D   7 D

2
1 wife   3 invitation   5 Sunday
2 daughter   4 brother   6 school

3
1 flat   3 know   5 meet
2 right   4 name   6 juice

4
1 from   3 friend   5 **A**nything
2 class   4 break   6 m**e**di**u**m

UNIT 2
VOCABULARY My home
1
hn centre cdki city pl flats qw house br north ol road dw south ky park mn village as

2
1 village   4 house   7 park
2 north   5 road   8 flats
3 south   6 city

GRAMMAR Present simple
3
1 walk   3 live   5 have   7 knows
2 takes   4 has   6 like

4
1 knows   3 know   5 have   7 lives
2 live   4 like   6 takes

5
1 like   3 have   5 likes
2 has   4 lives   6 knows

GRAMMAR Present simple questions: *do you ... ?*
6
1 Do you like   3 Do you have   6 Do you walk
2 Who do you   4 Where do
   live   5 Do you know

7
a 3   b 2   c 5   d 4   e 6   f 1

8
1 Do you live with your mother and father?
2 Do you like my husband's village?
3 Do you have a big house?
4 Where do you live?
5 Who do you know here?
6 Where do you have a flat?

DEVELOPING CONVERSATIONS And you?
9
1 I'm twenty. And you?   2
   I'm eighteen.   3
   How old are you?   1
2 I'm great.   3
   Fine, thanks. And you?   2
   How are you?   1
3 Caleb. And you?   2
   Marianna.   3
   What's your name?   1

10
1 I'm OK.   3 Near the park.   5 No, it's very
2 Suki.   4 Yes, a sister.   big.

LISTENING
11
1, 4, 6, 7

12
1 on Venice Road   3 walks   5 small
2 their school   4 a flat   6 friends

Vocabulary Jobs

1
1. bus driver, a
2. mum, d
3. nurse, h
4. retired, f
5. student, g
6. teacher, b
7. waiter, c
8. work in an office, e

Grammar Present simple: *don't (do not)*

2
1. I don't live in a flat.
2. They don't like big cities.
3. We don't go to school.
4. You don't have a job.
5. They don't work in an office.

3
Students' own answers

Grammar Plural / no plural

4
✓ 1, 2, 5, 8, 9
✗ 3, 4, 6, 7

5
1. nurses
2. children
3. students
4. ✗
5. people
6. flats
7. ✗
8. drinks
9. mums
10. areas

6
1. is
2. time
3. are
4. houses
5. are
6. flats

Reading

7
1. Canada
2. England
3. Sweden
4. Poland

8
1 F 2 T 3 F 4 T 5 F 6 F 7 T 8 F

Developing writing Writing a description of yourself

9
1 a 2 c 3 d 4 b 5 e 6 g 7 f

10
1. Acacia Gonzales
2. 19
3. Mexico
4. Comitán
5. Chiapas
6. south
7. my mother and father
8. Instituto Tecnológico

11
Students' own answers

Vocabulary Food and drinks

1
1. orange juice
2. salad
3. drinks
4. coffee cake
5. meat

2
Across
1. juice
3. fish
5. meat
Down
2. chicken
3. fruit
4. salad

Grammar *like / don't like*

3
1. don't like
2. love
3. like
4. don't like
5. like
6. love

4
Students' own answers

5
1. it
2. them
3. them
4. it
5. it
6. them

Developing conversations Ordering food

6
1. Anything else with your fish? W
2. Are you ready to order? W
3. Chips, please. C
4. The fish, please. C
5. How much is a salad? C
6. And you? W
7. It's ten pounds. W
8. Oh! No, thanks. C
9. With rice or chips? W
10. Yes. A burger with chips for me. C

7
W: Are you ready to order?
C: Yes. A burger with chips for me.
W: And you?
C: The fish, please.
W: With rice or chips?
C: Chips, please.
W: Anything else with your fish?
C: How much is a salad?
W: It's ten pounds.
C: Oh! No, thanks.

Listening

9
1 b 2 d 3 c 4 a

10
1 F 2 T 3 T 4 T 5 F 6 F 7 F 8 T

Pronunciation /z/ and /s/

11
/z/ and /s/

12
/z/: doctors, does, hours, lives
/s/: bus driver, flats, house, south

Vocabulary Builder Quiz 2

1
1 PL 2 PL 3 P 4 P 5 PL 6 P 7 P

2
1. expensive
2. person
3. carrot
4. ice cream
5. minute
6. dog

3
1. vegetables
2. south
3. dad
4. small
5. far
6. chips

4
1. live
2. hours
3. area
4. house
5. retired
6. university

138 OUTCOMES

UNIT 3

VOCABULARY Adjectives

1
1 d 2 b 3 a 4 c

2
1 difficult 4 hungry 7 tired
2 expensive 5 married 8 well
3 great 6 nice

3
1 a, hot 3 an, old 5 an, expensive
2 a, big 4 a, hungry 6 a, tired

PRONUNCIATION Saying words together

4
1 an expensive 3 an English
2 an orange 4 an old

GRAMMAR Negatives with be

6
1 's not 3 're not 5 's not
2 're not 4 'm not

7
1 's not 3 's not 5 'm not
2 're not 4 're not

8
1 's not 2 're not 3 're not 4 's not 5 'm not

LISTENING

9
1 c 2 d 3 a 4 b

10
a 3 b 1 c 4 d 2

11
1 very well 3 hot
2 expensive 4 very good, difficult

DEVELOPING CONVERSATIONS Responding to news

13
Good news: She's very well, thanks. It's very nice. The other students are great.
Bad news: It's very cold here. My chicken's not hot. His job is difficult.

14
1 It's very cold here. 4 My chicken's not hot.
2 His job is difficult. 5 The other students are great.
3 She's very well, thanks. 6 It's very nice.

15
1 I'm sorry. 3 Oh, good. 5 Oh, good.
2 I'm sorry. 4 I'm sorry. 6 Oh, good.

VOCABULARY go, take, want

1
1 takes 3 wants 5 takes 7 takes
2 goes 4 goes 6 wants

2
1 takes 5 goes 9 goes
2 goes 6 wants 10 goes
3 takes 7 goes 11 takes
4 takes 8 wants

GRAMMAR Present simple: doesn't

3
1 He doesn't like fish.
2 Leo doesn't know my teacher.
3 The train doesn't take a long time.
4 My brother doesn't want to go to the party.
5 The bus doesn't go to the city.
6 She doesn't live in a new house.

4
1 She doesn't take the train.
2 He doesn't like his hotel.
3 Maria doesn't go shopping every day.
4 My mother doesn't have a car.
5 It doesn't take long to walk to school.
6 The number 10 bus doesn't go near my gym.

5
1 wants, doesn't want 3 takes, doesn't like
2 has, doesn't have 4 takes, doesn't take

GRAMMAR Present simple questions: does

6
1 f 2 c 3 d 4 a 5 b 6 e

7
1 Why 3 How 5 What
2 Where 4 What 6 Who

8
1 How long does the bus take?
2 What does your brother do?
3 Where does Steven work?
4 When does she go to the gym?
5 Where does he go at two o'clock?

READING

9
Lucia and Vincenzo

10
1 Does 4 Does 7 Is
2 What 5 Does 8 Does
3 Where 6 How much

11
1 a 2 b 3 a 4 b 5 b 6 b 7 a 8 a

VOCABULARY Things

1
Across
2 food 4 map 6 towel 7 shoes 8 coat
Down
1 soap 3 dictionary 5 pen

2
1 map 2 pen 3 money 4 brush 5 food

DEVELOPING CONVERSATIONS Asking for help in conversation

3
1 Sorry   3 Can   5 How
2 say   4 again   6 English

GRAMMAR *a* and *any*

5
Do you have a ...?: book, brush, coat, map, mobile
Do you have any ...?: bags, food, local money, other shoes, toothpaste

6
1 any   4 anything   7 any   10 any
2 anything   5 a   8 any   11 any
3 any   6 a   9 any

7
Students' own answers

DEVELOPING WRITING Writing an email

8
1 b   2 a

9
1 b   2 d   3 f   4 a   5 c   6 g   7 e

10
Students' own answers

VOCABULARY BUILDER QUIZ 3

1
1 a book   3 shopping   5 married
2 clothes   4 a shower   6 holiday

2
1 room   3 phone   5 charger
2 time   4 paste   6 time

3
1 very   3 difficult   5 local   7 adjectives
2 hungry   4 other   6 expensive

4
1 b   2 e   3 d   4 f   5 c   6 a

UNIT 4
VOCABULARY Places

1
1 pool   3 station   5 market
2 machine   4 park   6 shop

2
1 church   4 restaurant   7 cinema
2 café   5 park   8 hotel
3 hospital   6 bank   9 market

3
1 church   5 hotel   9 restaurant
2 supermarket 6 cinema   10 car park
3 café   7 bank
4 hospital   8 park

GRAMMAR *Is there ... ? / There's ...*

4
1 Is there   4 There's   7 There's
2 There's   5 there isn't 8 Is there
3 there isn't 6 Is there

5
1 Is there   3 Is there   5 Is there
2 there isn't 4 there isn't 6 there's

VOCABULARY EXTRA Prepositions and directions

7
1 on   4 at the end   7 down
2 next to   5 near   8 on the left
3 in   6 on the corner

8
1 down   3 near   5 in   7 on
2 next   4 on   6 at   8 right

DEVELOPING CONVERSATIONS *called*

9
1 town   3 restaurant   5 café
2 clothes shop   4 cinema

LISTENING

10
1 c   2 b   3 a

11
1 e   2 d   3 b   4 f   5 c   6 a

PRONUNCIATION Syllable stress

1
1 1 syllable   3 3 syllables   5 4 syllables
2 2 syllables   4 2 syllables   6 1 syllable

2
1 station   3 market
2 hospital   4 supermarket

VOCABULARY Days and times of day

3
1 Sunday   4 Wednesday   7 Saturday
2 Monday   5 Thursday
3 Tuesday   6 Friday

4
1 night   3 yesterday   5 tomorrow
2 afternoon   4 today

5
1 morning   3 afternoon   5 night
2 from   4 evening   6 to

6
1 Tuesday
2 Today: Saturday   Yesterday: Friday
3 Tomorrow: Wednesday   Yesterday: Monday

GRAMMAR Adverbs of frequency

7
100%   always
75%   normally / usually
25%   sometimes
0%   never

8
1 always   4 usually / normally
2 sometimes   5 usually / normally
3 never

9
Students' own answers

140 OUTCOMES

Reading

10
b

11
1 usually 2 always 3 normally 4 always

12
1 She's from Nova Scotia, Canada.
2 She's a teacher.
3 In a school (in a small village).
4 In the city. / At a supermarket called Sobey's and clothes shop called Winners.
5 At 4 (in the afternoon).
6 Fresh fruit.
7 Her friends.
8 Her job.
9 Weekends.

Grammar Can …?

1
a 5   b 4   c 6   d 1   e 3   f 2

2
1 Can I   3 Can you   5 Can you
2 Can you   4 Can I   6 Can I

3
1 Can we have a break?
2 Can we have ten more minutes?
3 Can we have food in the class?
4 Can you close the window?
5 Can you do Exercise 9?
6 Can you help me?
7 Can you wait a minute?

Vocabulary Classroom verbs

4
1 c   2 f   3 e   4 d/h   5 b   6 a   7 d/h   8 g

5
1 leave   3 Come   5 Use
2 Turn on   4 write   6 share

Developing Writing A note describing where you live

6
1 but   2 but   3 and   4 and   5 but   6 and

7
1 c   2 b

8
1 20 Garden Road   4 at 10 in the morning
2 take the train   5 down the road
3 museum there called

9
Students' own answers

10
Students' own answers

Vocabulary Builder Quiz 4

1
1 a film   3 a shop   5 your tablet
2 $5   4 English

2
1 machine   3 shop   5 name
2 station   4 park

3
1 b   2 d   3 a   4 c   5 e

4
1 third   3 evening   5 today
2 mosque   4 book

5
1 many   3 called   5 understand
2 right   4 closed

UNIT 5
Vocabulary Getting there

1
get: a taxi, home, off the train, the metro, the red line, to work
go: home, to work
take: a taxi, the metro, the red line
walk: home, to work
change: trains
wait: for the bus

2
1 get, walk   3 go   5 get
2 Take, change   4 wait, take

Grammar Are there … ? / There are …

3
1 c   2 a   3 b   4 c   5 b   6 a   7 b   8 b

5
1 Are there   3 There's   5 There are
2 a   4 Is there a   6 any

6
Students' own answers

7
Students' own answers

Developing Conversations best

8
1 It's far from here. It's best to take a taxi.
2 Where's the best place to see some interesting art?
3 What's the best area in the city?
4 Is that the best café to sit and have a coffee?
5 Where's the best place to go swimming?

Listening

9
1 b   2 e   3 c   4 a   5 d

10
1 T 2 F 3 F 4 T 5 F 6 T 7 T 8 F
9 T 10 F

Vocabulary Buying tickets
1
1 change trains
2 pay by card
3 first class
4 the next train
5 return
6 second class
7 single

2
Across
2 card 4 machine 5 cash
Down
1 ticket 3 receipt

3
1 change 4 machine 7 next
2 pay, card 5 enter 8 receipt
3 first class 6 return

Pronunciation /k/ and /s/
4
/k/ and /s/

5
/k/: card, cash, costs, first class
/s/: centre, city, office, receipt

Reading
7
Advert 2

8
1 a 2 a 3 b 4 a 5 b 6 a

Developing Conversations Where are you going?
10
Conversation 1: d   Conversation 4: b
Conversation 2: a   Conversation 5: c
Conversation 3: e

Grammar Talking about plans: I'm / We're going
1
Where: to the bank, to the market, to the museum, home
What: to see some interesting art, to go swimming
When: this evening, now

2
1 I'm going 3 're going 5 'm going
2 're going 4 'm going 6 're going

3
1 'm going to play 4 're going to see
2 're going to have 5 'm going to eat
3 'm going to meet 6 're going to stay

4
Students' own answers

Grammar Asking about plans: going and doing
5
1 going 2 going 3 doing 4 going 5 doing

6
1 Where are you going 3 Are you going
2 What time are you going 4 What are you doing

Developing Writing Writing a text message
7
1 He 2 It's 3 She's 4 They

8
1 She 2 He 3 They 4 It

9
b

10
1 tonight 3 Deadpool 2 5 eight
2 the cinema 4 the metro

11
Students' own answers

12
Students' own answers

Vocabulary Builder Quiz 5
1
1 o'clock 3 cash 5 passengers
2 outside 4 main

2
1 flight 3 return 5 views
2 line 4 journey

3
1 every 3 a long time 5 some help
2 second class 4 work

4
1 home 3 football 5 platform
2 card 4 museum

5
1 d 2 c 3 a 4 b 5 e

UNIT 6
Vocabulary Problems
1
1 late 3 rain 5 tired
2 noise 4 no-one 6 traffic

2
1 wrong 4 rain 7 late
2 traffic 5 no-one 8 nowhere
3 noise 6 tired 9 a problem

Grammar Past simple: irregular verbs
3
1 was 3 had 5 did
2 were 4 went

4
1 were 4 was 7 did
2 had 5 was, did, went
3 went 6 was

Developing Conversations Don't worry / That's OK
5
1 That 3 OK 5 That's
2 Don't 4 worry

142 OUTCOMES

READING

6
b

7
1 T   2 F   3 T   4 T   5 F   6 F

8
1 Turkey
2 six hours and thirty minutes
3 Via Laietana
4 La Rambla
5 evening

VOCABULARY Hotels and checking in

1
1 check out   4 breakfast   7 password
2 bag   5 key   8 passport
3 room   6 lift

2
1 address, number   5 lift
2 passport   6 booking
3 breakfast, check out   7 password
4 key   8 bag

GRAMMAR Regular past simple endings

3
verb + -d: liked, loved, shared
verb + -ed: rained, stayed, talked

4
1 liked   3 rained   5 talked
2 stayed   4 loved   6 shared

PRONUNCIATION Past simple forms

5
different
/t/: liked
/d/: rained
/id/: visited

6
/t/: talked, walked, watched
/d/: danced, shared, stayed
/id/: needed, started, wanted

GRAMMAR Past simple negatives

8
1 didn't have   4 didn't see   7 didn't go
2 didn't like   5 didn't talk   8 weren't
3 didn't rain   6 wasn't   9 didn't

9
1 It didn't rain in my city on Friday.
2 On my trip, I didn't see interesting art.
3 At school, I didn't talk to my English teacher.
4 I didn't have a party last weekend.
5 On my holiday, I didn't like the local food.
6 I didn't do a lot of work today.
7 On my bus journey, there wasn't a lot of noise.
8 I didn't go shopping yesterday.

10
Students' own answers

LISTENING

11
3

12
1 f   2 b   3 h   4 a   5 d   6 i   7 c
8 g   9 e

GRAMMAR Past simple questions

1
1 did you have   4 did you see   7 did you do
2 did you go   5 did you get   8 Did you go
3 did you leave   6 Did you go

2
Students' own answers

3
1 did you buy, c   4 did you get up, e
2 did you live, a   5 did you study, f
3 did you go, d   6 Did you stay, b

GRAMMAR REVIEW: Past simple

4
1 There was a problem at the café.
2 We weren't late for class.
3 I had breakfast at home.
4 They didn't go to the museum.
5 We did a lot of interesting things.
6 When did you get home?
7 I didn't like Rome.
8 We stayed in a great hostel.
9 Did you talk to the doctor? / Did the doctor talk to you?
10 Where did you have dinner?

5
1 was
2 went
3 did you have, didn't have, was
4 did you stay, stayed
5 was, weren't
6 Did you like, shared
7 did you see, didn't go, walked

DEVELOPING WRITING Writing a review

6
1 to   3 were   5 We're
2 their   4 two   6 there

7
b

8
Students' own answers

9
Students' own answers

VOCABULARY BUILDER QUIZ 6

1
1 music   3 flight   5 tour
2 no-one   4 password

2
1 traffic   3 booking   5 key
2 hungry   4 band

3
1 party
2 your bed
3 exercise
4 weather
5 problem

4
1 passport
2 star
3 lake
4 rain
5 lift

5
1 b   2 d   3 a   4 e   5 c

NATIONAL GEOGRAPHIC
LEARNING

National Geographic Learning,
a Cengage Company

Outcomes Beginner Student's Book / Workbook Combo Split A
**Hugh Dellar and Andrew Walkley;
Kelly Phillips**

Vice President, Editorial Director: John McHugh

Executive Editor: Siân Mavor

Editorial Project Manager: Laura Brant

Development Editors: Stephanie Parker; Clare Shaw

Head of Strategic Marketing EMEA ELT: Charlotte Ellis

Product Marketing Manager: Victoria Taylor

Head of Production and Design: Mike Burggren

Content Project Manager: Ruth Moore

Manufacturing Manager: Eyvett Davis

Cover Design: Lisa Trager

Interior Design and Composition: emc design ltd.

© 2019 Cengage Learning, Inc.

ALL RIGHTS RESERVED. No part of this work covered by the copyright herein may be reproduced or distributed in any form or by any means, except as permitted by U.S. copyright law, without the prior written permission of the copyright owner.

"National Geographic", "National Geographic Society" and the Yellow Border Design are registered trademarks of the National Geographic Society ® Marcas Registradas

For permission to use material from this text or product,
submit all requests online at **cengage.com/permissions**
Further permissions questions can be emailed to
permissionrequest@cengage.com

Student's Book and Workbook Split A
ISBN: 978-0-357-04344-8

National Geographic Learning
Cheriton House
North Way
Andover
UK
SP10 5BE

Locate your local office at **international.cengage.com/region**

Visit National Geographic Learning online at **ELTNGL.com**
Visit our corporate website at **www.cengage.com**

CREDITS
Although every effort has been made to contact copyright holders before publication, this has not always been possible. If contacted, the publisher will undertake to rectify any errors or omissions at the earliest opportunity.

Photos
Cover AllisonGinadaio/iStock/Getty Images.
Front Matter
2 (tl) AshTproductions/Shutterstock.com; (tl) Philippe LEJEANVRE/Moment/Getty Images; (cl) Adrian Buck/Alamy Stock Photo; (cl) AllisonGinadaio/iStock/Getty Images; (bl) Skreidzeleu/Shutterstock.com; (bl) nui7711/Shutterstock.com; **4** (tl) wavebreakmedia/Shutterstock.com; (tl) Barry Winiker/Getty Images; (cl) Golubovy/Shutterstock.com; (cl) Marcos Mesa Sam Wordley/Shutterstock.com; (bl) Harry KiiM/Shutterstock.com; (bl) Ververidis Vasilis/Shutterstock.com;
6 (tl) AshTproductions/Shutterstock.com; (tr) Mohd Hafiez Mohd Razali/EyeEm/Getty Images; (c1) Standard Studio/Shutterstock.com; (c2) Iakov Filimonov/Shutterstock.com; (cl) Pietus/Shutterstock.com; (cr) Carlos Banyuls/Shutterstock.com; (bl) Monkey Business Images/Shutterstock.com; (br) WAYHOME studio/Shutterstock.com; **7** (tl) Klaus Tiedge/Blend Images/Getty Images; (cl) Monkey Business Images/Shutterstock.com; (bl) AP Images/Jonathan Brady; (br) Jorge Salcedo/Shutterstock.com; **8** (t) Greg Elms/Lonely Planet Images/Getty Images; (cr1) Michael Ochs Archives/Getty Images; (cr2) DIMITAR DILKOFF/AFP/Getty Images; (cr3) DEA PICTURE LIBRARY/De Agostini/Getty Images; **10** (tc1) Tetiana Yurchenko/Shutterstock.com; (tc2) Toronto-Images.Com/Shutterstock.com; (tr1) monticello/Shutterstock.com; (tr2) Min C. Chiu/Shutterstock.com; (tr3) MakaBaka/Shutterstock.com; (c) REPORTERS ASSOCIES/Gamma-Rapho/Getty Images; **12** lechatnoir/E+/Getty Images; **14** (tl) Philippe LEJEANVRE/Moment/Getty Images; (tr) Evelyn Chavez/Shutterstock.com; (cl) Monkey Business Images/Shutterstock.com; (cr) all_about_people/Shutterstock.com; (bl) tazzymoto/Shutterstock.com; (br) Monkey Business Images/Shutterstock.com; **15** (tl) steve estvanik/Shutterstock.com; (cl) macroworld/E+/Getty Images; (c) Claudia Totir/Moment/Getty Images; (cr) Ryan McGinnis/Alamy Stock Photo; (bl) Serg Zastavkin/Shutterstock.com; (br)

Printed in China by RR Donnelley
Print Number: 01 Print Year: 2019

Rostislav Glinsky/Shutterstock.com; **16** (tl) Rostislav Glinsky/Shutterstock.com; (tc) Philippe LEJEANVRE/Moment/Getty Images; (tr) Xiao Lng Fng/EyeEm/Getty Images; (cl) Stefanie Sudek-Mensch/STOCK4B/Getty Images; (c) Mehaniq/Shutterstock.com; (c) Planet Observer/UIG/Getty Images; (cr) Convery flowers/Alamy Stock Photo; (br) Juanmonino/E+/Getty Images; **18** (cl) coward_lion/Getty images; (c1) SolStock/E+/Getty Images; (c2) Patrick Fraser/Corbis/Getty Images; (cr1) Reza Estakhrian/Stone/Getty Images; (cr2) Hill Street Studios/Blend Images/Getty Images; (bl) Oleg Nikishin/Photonica World/Getty Images; (bc) Jeff Greenberg/Universal Images Group/Getty Images; (br1) Monkey Business Images/Shutterstock.com; (br2) Monkey Business Images/Shutterstock.com; **19** (bl1) alynst/E+/Getty Images; (bl2) NadiaRaigel/Moment/Getty Images; (br1) CraigRJD/E+/Getty Images; (br2) Ebtikar/Shutterstock.com; **21** (cl) Poplis, Paul/Foodcollection/Getty Images; (c1) Creativ Studio Heinemann/Westend61/Getty Images; (c2) Ivan/Moment/Getty Images; (cr1) Timolina/Shutterstock.com; (cr2) Valery Evlakhov/Shutterstock.com; espies/Shutterstock.com; (bl) Baloncici/Shutterstock.com; (bc) Tim Chong/EyeEm/Getty Images; (br) Dmitry Lityagin/Shutterstock.com; **22** Bogdan Khmelnytskyi/Shutterstock.com; **26** (tl) zhu difeng/Shutterstock.com; (tr) Christinlola/Dreamstime LLC; (cl1) eakkachai halang/Shutterstock.com; (cl2) LightField Studios/Shutterstock.com; (c) ps-42/Shutterstock.com; (cr) nikkytok/Shutterstock.com; (br) tuaindeed/Shutterstock.com; **27** (tl) Bread and Butter Productions/Photodisc/Getty Images; (cl) Juice Images Ltd/Getty Images; (cr) Adrian Buck/Alamy Stock Photo; (bl) Alyona Mandrik/Shutterstock.com; (br) Ronnie Kaufman/Larry Hirshowitz/Getty Images; **28** (tl) Ben Bloom/Getty Images; (tr) Jihan Abdalla/Blend Images/Getty Images; (cl) Yuriy Melnikov/EyeEm/Getty Images; (cr) Jonathan Kingston/National Geographic Creative; **30** Paul Rushton/Alamy Stock Photo; **31** (tl) Jane Williams/Alamy Stock Photo; (tr) Takahiko Katayama/Alamy Stock Photo; (cl) Hero Images/Getty Images; (cr) Paul Doyle/Alamy Stock Photo; **32** (t) IB Photography/Shutterstock.com; (tl1) sagarsubhashkalal/Shutterstock.com; (tl2) joserpizarro/Shutterstock.com; (tc) slobo/E+/Getty Images; (tr1) Voronin76/Shutterstock.com; (tr2) mauritius images GmbH/Alamy Stock Photo; (cl1) elenovsky/Shutterstock.com; (cl2) A. Aleksandravicius/Shutterstock.com; (cl3) Tewan Banditrukkanka/Shutterstock.com; (cl4) Photo Melon/Shutterstock.com; (c1) bjphotographs/Shutterstock.com; (c2) vitec/Shutterstock.com; (c3) Le Do/Shutterstock.com; (c4) jocic/Shutterstock.com; (c5) Prachaya Roekdeethaweesab/Shutterstock.com; (c6) Sergio Azenha/Alamy Stock Photo; (cr1) Kartinkin77/Shutterstock.com; (cr2) Maliflower73/Shutterstock.com; (cr3) grynold/Shutterstock.com; (cr4) zoff/Shutterstock.com; (bl) GOLFX/Shutterstock.com; (bc) Tetra Images/Getty Images; (br) JodiJacobson/E+/Getty Images; **33** (tl) MvanCaspel/Shutterstock.com; (cl) Monkey Business Images/Shutterstock.com; (c) Rafael Dias Katayama/Shutterstock.com; (bl) Capricorn Studio/Shutterstock.com; (br) Elder Pinto/Shutterstock.com; **34** (tl) Luís Henrique Boucault/Moment/Getty Images; (tr) Kumar Sriskandan/Alamy Stock Photo; (c) Rod Edwards/Alamy Stock Photo; **36** Frank Carter/Lonely Planet Images/Getty Images; **37** (bl) Gary C. Tognoni/Shutterstock.com; (br) Jane Sweeney/AWL Images/Getty Images; (br) saoirse2013/Shutterstock.com; **38** Jake Lyell/Alamy Stock Photo; **40** Mikhail Gnatkovskiy/Shutterstock.com; **42** (tl) georgeclerk/E+/Getty Images; (tr) Monkey Business Images/Shutterstock.com; (cl1) Stokkete/Shutterstock.com; (cl2) StreetVJ/Shutterstock.com; (cl3) Bill Roque/Shutterstock.com; (cr1) Artur Bogacki/Shutterstock.com; (cr2) Trusov/Shutterstock.com; (br) ANURAK PONGPATIMET/Shutterstock.com; **43** (tl) Anirut Thailand/Shutterstock.com; (cl) Ryan McVay/Photodisc/Getty Images; (cr) Skreidzeleu/Shutterstock.com; (b) SasinTipchai/Shutterstock.com; **44** Iain Masterton/Alamy Stock Photo; **46** (cr1) travelview/Shutterstock.com; (cr2) The Asahi Shimbun/Getty Images; (b) John Keates/Alamy Stock Photo; **47** travelview/Shutterstock.com; **48** Paul Davey/EyeEm/Getty Images; **50** (tr1) AriPaii/Shutterstock.com; (tr2) DrimaFilm/Shutterstock.com; (cl1) Richard Levine/Alamy Stock Photo; (cl2) Eddie Gerald/Alamy Stock Photo; (cr1) Nejron Photo/Shutterstock.com; (cr2) Dave and Les Jacobs/Blend Images/Getty Images; (bl) GaudiLab/Shutterstock.com; (br) nui7711/Shutterstock.com; **51** (tl) Aleksandra Suzi/Shutterstock.com; (cl1) siridhata/Shutterstock.com; (cl2) Serge Ka/Shutterstock.com; (c) Rawpixel.com/Shutterstock.com; (cr) Jack Frog/Shutterstock.com; (b) Galina Gordeeva/Shutterstock.com; **52** (tl) David Vilaplana/Alamy Stock Photo; (tr) Parilov/Shutterstock.com; **53** (tl) Naum Chayer/Alamy Stock Photo; (tr) Jetta Productions/Blend Images/Getty Images; **54** Paul Kingsley/Alamy Stock Photo; **55** (tr) Robert Francis/robertharding/Getty Images; (cr) age fotostock/Superstock; **56** JeffG/Alamy Stock Photo; **58** (tl) Chicago Tribune/Getty Images; (tc) Pablo Charlón/Getty Images; (tr) Hisham Ibrahim/Getty Images; **80** (tl) John Gress Media Inc/Shutterstock.com; (tc) Pictorial Press Ltd/Alamy Stock Photo; (tr) AGIF/Shutterstock.com; (cl) Kevin Mazur/One Love Manchester/Getty Images; (cl) pdrocha/Shutterstock.com; (c) NASA; (cr1) duncan1890/iStock/Getty Images; (cr2) Peter Horree/Alamy Stock Photo; (cr3) NurPhoto/Getty Images

97 (tl) © Estrada Anton/Shutterstock.com; **103** (tl) © meunierd/Shutterstock.com; **109** (tl) © gpointstudio/Shutterstock.com; **115** (tl) © Willy Barton/Shutterstock.com; **121** (tl) © TZIDO SUN/Shutterstock.com; **127** (tl) © Alf Ribeiro/Shutterstock.com; **96** (bl) © VGstockstudio/Shutterstock.com; **96** (br) © Hero Images/Getty Images; **97** (tl) © FS Productions/Blend Images/Getty Images; **97** (tl 1) © fatihhoca/E+/Getty Images; **97** (cl) © LightField Studios/Shutterstock.com; **97** (cr 1) © Beau Lark/Corbis/Getty Images; **97** (bl) © Monkey Business Images/Shutterstock.com; **97** (c) © HannaMonika/Shutterstock.com; **97** (cl) © Charlotte Purdy/Shutterstock.Com; **97** (tl 3) © Iakov Filimonov/Shutterstock.com; **97** (cr 2) © Kamil Macniak/Shutterstock.com; **97** (br 1) © WAYHOME studio/Shutterstock.com; **97** (br 2) © Odua Images/Shutterstock.com; **99** (tl) © Monkey Business Images/Shutterstock.com; **99** (cl) © oneinchpunch/Shutterstock.com; **99** (bl) © Tetiana Chernykova/Shutterstock.com; **100** (bl) © Odua Images/Shutterstock.com; **102** (br) © Milan Gonda/Shutterstock.com; **104** (tl) © Monkey Business Images/Shutterstock.com; **104** (tl) © YAKOBCHUK VIACHESLAV/Shutterstock.com; **104** (cl 1) © LightField Studios/Shutterstock.com; **104** (cr 1) © Syda Productions/Shutterstock.com; **104** (cl 2) © Alliance/Shutterstock.com; **104** (cr 2) © Gladskikh Tatiana/Shutterstock.com; **104** (bl) © Zurijeta/Shutterstock.com; **104** (br) © Minerva Studio/Shutterstock.com; **105** (bl) © Jenkedco/Shutterstock.com; **108** (tl) © Milan Stojanović/Dreamstime.com; **108** (tl) © Jackbluee/Dreamstime.com; **108** (cl) © John Arehart/Shutterstock.com; **108** (cr) © Lestertair/Shutterstock.com; **108** (bl) © olaser/E+/Getty Images; **108** (br) © Kosim Shukurov/Shutterstock.com; **109** (tl) © Nick Fox/Shutterstock.com; **109** (tl) © g-stockstudio/Shutterstock.com; **109** (bl) © Monkey Business Images/Shutterstock.com; **109** (br) © Roman Babakin/Shutterstock.com; **110** (tl) © Gabi Moisa/Shutterstock.com; **110** (cl) © Blend Images - KidStock/Brand X Pictures/Getty Images; **110** (bl) © Diego Cervo/Shutterstock.com; **112** (tl) © bitt24/Shutterstock.com; **112** (tc) © slobo/E+/Getty Images; **112** (tl) © sergign/Shutterstock.com; **112** (cl) © Nadezda/Shutterstock.com; **112** (cr) © Karkas/Shutterstock.com; **112** (bl) © Robert Red2000/Shutterstock.com; **112** (bc) © Terrance Emerson/Shutterstock.com; **112** (br) © Vangelis_Vassalakis/Shutterstock.com; **114** (tl) © Stuart Monk/Shutterstock.com; **114** (br) © Shuang Li/Shutterstock.com; **114** (tc) © Alastair Wallace/Shutterstock.com; **114** (cl) © VTT Studio/Shutterstock.com; **114** (c1) © Spotmatik Ltd/Shutterstock.com; **114** (c2) © Corepics VOF/Shutterstock.com; **114** (cr) © Peter Zurek/Shutterstock.com; **114** (bl) © Syda Productions/Shutterstock.com; **114** (bc 1) © Konstantin Romanov/Shutterstock.com; **114** (bc 2) © Kheng Guan Toh/Shutterstock.com; **115** (tl) © Gecko Studio/Shutterstock.com; **115** (b) © Bai-Bua's Dad/Shutterstock.com; **115** (tl) © Kingapl/Shutterstock.com; **117** (bc) © Loop Images/Universal Images Group/Getty Images; **119** (bl) © puhhha/Shutterstock.com; **121** (tl 1) © Takashi Images/Shutterstock.com; **121** (tl 2) © Daniel Hernanz Ramos/Moment/Getty Images; **121** (cr) © serdjophoto/Shutterstock.com; **121** (br 1) © Henryk T. Kaiser/Photolibrary/Getty Images; **121** (br 2) © Paolo Paradiso/Shutterstock.com; **122** (tl) © ICP/incamerastock/Alamy Stock Photo; **122** (tc) © PR Image Factory/Shutterstock.com; **122** (tl) © Gordon Bell/Shutterstock.com; **122** (bl) © Ceri Breeze/Shutterstock.com; **122** (cl) © Andrey_Popov/Shutterstock.com; **123** (tl) © oksana.perkins/Shutterstock.com; **123** (cr) © Sven Hansche/Shutterstock.com; **123** (bl) © SL-Photography/Shutterstock.com; **125** (cl) © Coast-to-Coast/iStock Editorial/Getty Images; **126** (tl) © Stokkete/Shutterstock.com; **126** (tl) © SpeedKingz/Shutterstock.com; **126** (cl) © Romolo Tavani/Shutterstock.com; **126** (cr) © Peshkova/Shutterstock.com; **126** (bl 2) © Elnur/Shutterstock.com; **126** (br) © Gubin Yury/Shutterstock.com; **127** (br) © Iakov Filimonov/Shutterstock.com; **128** (tl 1) © trebor/Alamy Stock Photo; **128** (tl 2) © S_Photo/Shutterstock.com; **128** (tl 3) © ©Berni/Shutterstock.com; **128** (cl 1) © Tatiana Bralnina/Shutterstock.com; **128** (cl 2) © PeJo29/iStock/Getty Images; **128** (bl 1) © Komar/Shutterstock.com; **128** (bl 3) © Rawpixel.com/Shutterstock.com; **128** (tl) © nhungboon/Shutterstock.com; **129** (tl) © Radu Bercan/Shutterstock.com; **129** (cr) © happymay/Shutterstock.com; **129** (br) © chuyuss/Shutterstock.com; **131** (cl) © SONNY TUMBELAKA/AFP/Getty Images; **40** (tl) © Dmitriy Shironosov/Alamy Stock Photo; **40** (tl) © LightField Studios/Shutterstock.com; **40** (cl) © Golubovy/Shutterstock.com; **40** (cr) © Monkey Business Images/Shutterstock.com

DVD videos
Video 1 photos (1) Bogdan Khmelnytskyi/Shutterstock.com; (3) Scott Hortop Life/Alamy Stock Photo; (5) arabianEye/Getty Images; Video 2 photos (2) MAHATHIR MOHD YASIN/Shutterstock.com; (4) Boston Globe/Getty Images; (5) Romankonovalov/Shutterstock.com; (7) Mikhail Gnatkovskiy/Shutterstock.com; (8) Simon Mayer/Shutterstock.com; Videos 3, 4 and 6 National Geographic; Video 5 Paulina Almazan

Illustrations
45 Clive Goodyer/Beehive Illustration; 8 (ml, bl), 9 Phil Hackett/Eye Candy Illustration; 13 Daniel Limon/Beehive Illustration; 16 (c) Dave Russell; 39 Gary Venn/Lemonade Illustration; 30 (bl) Dan Widdowson/The Bright Agency.

Acknowledgements
The publishers and authors would like to thank the following teachers who provided the feedback and user insights that have helped us develop *Outcomes* Beginner: Silvia Carchano Alcina, EOI Gandia, Gandia, Spain; Lara Alvarez, Newham College of Further Education, London, UK; David Byrne, EC London, London, UK; Sarah Donno, Edinburgh College, Edinburgh, UK; Eder Garces, EC London, London, UK; SoYeong Kim, EC London, London, UK; Luz Stella Hernández Ortiz, Universidad de La Sabana, Chia, Colombia; Melissa Perkins, EC London, London, UK

Authors' acknowledgements
Thanks to our editors Stephanie Parker, Dona Velluti, Laura Brant and Siân Mavor. Also thanks to John McHugh, Dennis Hogan, and NGL for their continued support and enthusiasm for the *Outcomes* series.
Thanks also to all the students we've taught over the years for providing more inspiration and insight than they ever realised. And to the colleagues we've taught alongside for their friendship, thoughts and assistance.